DRINK ME!

How to
CHOOSE, TASTE
and **ENJOY** *wine*

MATT WALLS

Quadrille
PUBLISHING

'We want the finest wines available to humanity. We want them here, and we want them now!'

WITHNAIL AND I

EDITORIAL DIRECTOR Anne Furniss
CREATIVE DIRECTOR Helen Lewis
PROJECT EDITOR Simon Davis
EDITOR Jamie Ambrose
DESIGNER Katherine Case
ILLUSTRATOR Katherine Case
PRODUCTION DIRECTOR Vincent Smith
PRODUCTION CONTROLLER James Finan

First published in 2012 by
Quadrille Publishing Limited
Alhambra House
27–31 Charing Cross Road
London WC2H 0LS
www.quadrille.co.uk

Text © copyright Matt Walls 2012
Design and layout © copyright
Quadrille Publishing Ltd 2012

Cataloguing in Publication Data: a catalogue record
for this book is available from the British Library.

ISBN 978 184949 140 2

Printed in China

INTRODUCTION

Over the years I've collected many books on wine. A few are weighty reference books; some are specialized guides to winemaking and the more technical elements of wine production. Several deal with subjects such as food-and-wine matching, grape varieties and buying guides. What I could never find was a concise book that covered all the things you really need to know in plain English: a guide for people who drink a bit and know a little but would like to know more. Hopefully this book will plug that gap.

Wine can be powerful stuff. I've seen a grown man cry just from tasting a great bottle. But it's not all a life-changing experience. Sometimes you just want a glass of something interesting while you chat with a friend, or wash down a burger: something to turn a plate of food into a meal. Few things in life can be enjoyed every day, give you a fabulous sensual thrill and are also good for you, so it's worth taking time to make sure you get the best out of every bottle. Open one bottle a week for the next 50 years, and you've only got around 2,500 bottles left. Make all of them count.

Why read this book?

This book will help you choose the right bottle for the right situation. You'll learn about the main wine types – still, sparkling, sweet, dry and fortified. How to get hold of the best bottles isn't the only thing you need to know; getting the most out of the wine once you've bought it is just as important. A few simple techniques will radically change the way a wine tastes once it's in your mouth. And there are ways of thinking about and talking about what you're tasting that will help you get more out of your bottle, from the most basic glugger to a venerable old vintage.

Wine by itself can bring a huge amount of enjoyment, but when you drink it with food, it makes a big difference – both to the taste of the wine and to the flavour of the food. Get the match right, and you bring out the best in both drink and dinner. We'll also look at the most well-known wine regions and what to expect from a typical example, so you'll know whether they might be the kind of thing you'd enjoy. This should give you enough info to start exploring (or avoiding) different regions, grape varieties or styles of wine.

If it's geological data, statistical information and the history of Greek wine amphorae you're looking for, then this might not be the book for you. But if you simply want to know which wines are safe to take to a prospective father-in-law's for lunch; how to tell what a wine tastes like by its grape variety; what the waiter wants to know when he asks if you want a wine decanted; and what different sherries taste like and why they will make you a happier person, then read on.

Start drinking the good stuff

Alcohol can be a wonderful substance and deserves to be celebrated. Would we drink wine if it tasted exactly the same but had no effect on the spirit? Of course, but it's even better like it is. It has a wonderfully predictable effect. The genie in the bottle loosens the tongue, relaxes the stiff upper lip, encourages laughter and precipitates conversation. The alcoholic component of wine is also vital to the way it tastes. It contributes body and texture, and adds a hint of warmth that provides complexity and length of flavour. It also helps to preserve wine as it ages.

And as well as alcohol, the enjoyment of wine also comes from nuances of flavours, the feel in the mouth, the way flavours change in the glass throughout the course of the bottle. Like music is to sound, and painting is to colour, wine is to flavour – and the flavours and aromas work together to create waves and layers of experience of varying intensity and subtlety. Like a piece of music, they can incite amazement, excitement, emotion; they can transport you to another place, if just for a moment.

It is that holy grail of the hedonistic pleasure that is both sustainable and healthy.

Because of the way wine matures and develops, most natural flavours can be found in it: herbs, spices, fruits, nuts, vegetables, dairy flavours, meaty flavours... you name it. And that's along with others you can't name. I'm still confronted from time to time with flavours in great wine I've never tasted before, aromas I've never smelled before. I can rarely, if ever, say the same for colours or sounds, even in the most stunning paintings or pieces of music. Wine is a bottomless box of delights.

The aims of this book are as follows: to demystify the topic and make it approachable; to give you the basic practical information you need in order to be able to explore the different types of wine you typically find in shops and restaurants, and to give you plenty of tricks and tips to get the most out of every bottle you open. Wine was once reserved for the richest in society. It's not any more. No one should allow old-fashioned attitudes to wine to stop them from enjoying the amazing experiences it has to offer. I want everyone to be able to get the same pleasure as I do from this amazing substance.

Needless to say, a modicum of moderation is the key to enjoying alcohol for the duration of a long and happy life. For ten years, I've been working in wine in a number of different guises, gradually tasting my way through every style at every level. For the past couple of years I've been managing a shop where I've been lucky enough to taste and share truly exceptional wines on a daily basis. There's not a single wine style I don't enjoy. They all have something to offer, as long as the quality is good. So don't put up with the average; the good stuff is within your reach. You just need to know how to get your hands on it.

BUYING, TASTING, DRINKING

PART 1

1

SO IT'S FERMENTED grape JUICE, RIGHT?

B ack in the mists of time, you used to get wine flavoured with herbs, spices and even lead, but nowadays if you're talking wine, you're talking grapes. Grapes are ideal for winemaking due to their high natural sugar content: it's the sugar that turns to alcohol. Grapes will also grow anywhere it's warm enough and there's a drop of water. The grapevine really is a pretty rugged creature. Given half a chance, it quickly takes hold and snakes around anything nearby. In fact, when growing grapes for wine, it's often a case of battling to control the vines' desire to grow like mad, so it's best to plant them in neat rows where they can be harvested easily. In large commercial vineyards, harvesting is often mechanized, conducted by peculiar machines with two long legs on tiny wheels that straddle a row of vines, shaking off grapes as they go. This isn't the best method. It reminds me of the time some friends and I made a night-time raid on a pick-your-own farm; we just scrabbled about in the dark trying to find strawberries. Some were delicious. Some were underripe. Some were rotten. Some were furry and squeaked...

GROWING
the grapes

For much the same reason, in the best estates grape-picking is still done by hand, which is gruelling work, and especially difficult in regions like Hermitage or Côte-Rôtie in France's Rhône Valley. There you're staggering up a 45-degree mountainside in 45-degree heat with a massive sack of grapes on your back. It's more expensive to employ a team of pickers to do this job, but at least you know only healthy, ripe grapes are going in the sack without any bird poo, snails or small furry animals (known as 'MOG' – *Material Other than Grapes*).

Grapevines tend to be tied along wires, in rows, and there are lots of different 'training systems' (I'll spare you details; it's boring). A curious thing about vines, though, is that they like it rough. So instead of giving each plant room to breathe, it's better to pack them in and make them fight each other to survive. This forces them to send their roots deep into the soil, picking up more nutrients along the way and making for better wine. Vines need water, but again, not too much; otherwise they get lazy and won't work hard. Mainly, they like infertile, well-drained soil.

It's amazing what grapevines will grow in. In France's Châteauneuf-du-Pape, the topsoil is covered in huge round stones called galets *that the vines push their way through.*

In Priorat, near Barcelona, there's no topsoil; they blow up the mountainside with dynamite, then smash it with bulldozers to give vines something to grow in. But grow they do, in the scorching heat, pushing their roots through solid rock.

Fungus, bugs and other nasties

Even the hardiest grapevine has natural enemies: diseases such as mildew or fungal rot, and the intriguingly named 'dead arm'. Most can be tackled with chemicals, or, even better, natural treatments. More vineyards are moving towards organic practices, but it's not easy – especially in cooler or damper climates.

It isn't just disease the vine-grower has to worry about. There are also pests, such as little worms and spiders that attack grapes or vines. Some are pretty serious, particularly phylloxera: a root-attacking louse that single-handedly nearly destroyed all the vineyards in Europe. This tiny aphid that feeds on vine roots was accidentally brought into Europe from North America in the second half of the nineteenth century.

North American vines are immune to phylloxera, but European vines aren't – and so this ravenous little insect rampaged through the vineyards of France, where it was first recorded in 1863, then made its way across Europe, destroying entire wine-producing regions at a frightening pace. By the late nineteenth century, phylloxera had reached almost all the Old World's winemaking countries. At the time, 2.5 million hectares of vineyards were destroyed – i.e. most of them. The future of winemaking in France, indeed Europe, hung in the balance.

Eventually, after many experiments (such as burying live toads under the vines) a cure was discovered: uproot a North American vine, chop off the growth above soil level, plant it in where you want it, then graft a European vine onto the stump. This way, its roots are immune from the pest and the vine keeps producing fruit.

COW HORNS AND MOON CYCLES: BIODYNAMICS Biodynamic viticulture is a bit like organics on acid. It's a practical/spiritual approach to farming set out in 1924 by Rudolf Steiner. Is it really the cow horn full of manure, buried in winter, then dug up and used as a spray the next year, that makes the difference to wine quality? Or is it simply that biodynamic winemakers pay more attention to their vines and work longer in the vineyard? Either way, biodynamic principles seem to lead to healthier vineyards and very lively wines.

HUNGRY BIRDS
Use netting, colourful kites or loud noises to keep them away

IN GERMANY, WILD BOAR HAVE BEEN KNOWN TO EAT ENTIRE CROPS
Kill 'em, skin 'em and eat 'em (along with a bottle of something rustic from the Languedoc...)

IN NORTH AMERICA, MICE AND VOLES EAT LEAVES AND SHOOTS
Set traps

IN CANADA, BEARS HAVE BEEN KNOWN TO ATTACK GRAPE-PICKERS
Scarper!

IN CALIFORNIA, DEER EAT VINE LEAVES
Erect electric fences to keep them out

IN SOUTH AFRICA, BABOONS MIGHT TRY AND EAT YOUR CROP
Put up extra-strong electric fences to keep these critters out

IN AUSTRALIA, KANGAROOS MUNCH SHOOTS
Surround the vines with barbed wire

IN FRANCE AND AUSTRALIA, RABBITS AND HARES EAT THE BARK AND LEAVES
Shoot or poison them

Bigger pests can also cause problems, as shown above. But if they can avoid all these hazards, and there's plenty of sun, grapevines are happy enough. Grapes need sunshine to ripen sufficiently, which is why they're planted on sites with good sun exposure, such as (in the northern hemisphere, at least) south-facing hillsides. In really hot places sometimes the opposite is true, and growers must keep vines from getting stressed. Often the most delicious wines are made in areas only just able to grow grapes, such as Bordeaux, Germany and Champagne.

Vines are often compared to people. They live for around 100 years if they're very lucky, but do their best work between 30 and 60 years old. When young, they're strong, vigorous and give lots of fruit. As they age, the amount of fruit lessens, but it's of a greater quality and value. At the very end, they give little in volume, yet the quality of what they produce is outstanding. And eventually they get too expensive to look after, so you get rid of them. Only joking, Granddad...

MAKING
the wine

In the northern hemisphere, harvest takes place around September/October, depending on the region, grape variety, wine style and growing season. If juice from a year's crop isn't blended with juice or wine from another year, you get a 'vintage' wine. The term doesn't refer to quality; only that the fruit that went into the wine was all from a single harvest. So, if the weather was good, it's a good vintage; if it was less favourable, it might be a vintage to avoid. A 'non-vintage' wine is one made by blending wines of different vintages before bottling.

Picking in hot climates is often done at night to keep the grapes in good condition, since a winery can be miles away, and grapes don't like being cooked in big metal trucks.

Once they arrive, the grapes are tipped into a crushing machine that breaks up the skins, pulp, and stalks. It's important not to crush the pips (or seeds, if you prefer), as these contain bitter oils and the wrong kind of tannin: a vaguely mysterious component we'll look at later that affects the texture and feel of a wine in the mouth. Grapes used to be crushed with human feet, which do a very effective job. Treading is still used to make some wines, particularly good-quality Port. Turns your legs purple for days, though – not a good look on the beach.

So, it's red grapes for red wine and green grapes for white wine?

Not always. Cut open a grape, red or green, and the flesh is a clear jelly. The colour of red grapes lies in the skins; to get red wine, pigment has to be extracted from the skins. This happens by leaving the juice in contact with the skins during fermentation.

It's possible to make white wine out of red grapes. After crushing, all skins are skimmed off the juice so the colour doesn't leach out, leaving it uncoloured. Rosé wines are made by leaving skins in the juice for a few hours to a couple of days, so that only a little colour is extracted. It's rarely legal to make rosé by blending red and white wine. With white wines, crushed grapes are then gently pressed to get a bit more juice, which is rich in flavour but potentially a little harsh if too much pressure is exerted. All of it then goes in a tank or barrel to ferment. With reds, the skins go in, too.

At this point a winemaker may decide to add tartaric acid (it occurs naturally in grapes) or sugar. Acid is added if the grapes weren't picked soon enough and their acidity level dropped as a result. Sugar is added if it was a cool growing season and the grapes didn't ripen, or if they were picked too early before enough natural sugar was produced. These adjustments are only legal in certain regions, however.

A number of other chemicals might be used, most notably sulphur dioxide (SO_2). This helps avoid oxidation, and its use is widespread, even in organic wines. Oxidation during the winemaking process can seriously impair the taste of the finished wine. Mind you, so can excess SO_2, so it needs to be used judiciously.

And now for the fermentation bit

Once the grape juice has been extracted, it's time for the magic ingredient, yeast: either super-efficient brewers' yeast or wild yeast. Ever notice the white, dusty stuff on grapes growing outside? That contains natural yeast. Many winemakers swear by it, but it isn't as effective as the manufactured stuff because it can be temperamental to use. Either way, it's bubbling time. The process works like this:

SUGAR + **YEAST** = **ALCOHOL** + **CARBON DIOXIDE (CO_2)**

Essentially, yeasts are dirty little fungi that munch through natural sugars in grape juice, farting CO_2 and weeing alcohol as they go. Nice. This delightful process turns sweet grape juice into less sweet but ultimately tastier wine. It normally takes a few weeks, during which you'll hear fizzing and see froth on top of the tank from CO_2 rising into the air. Fermentation time depends on temperature. The hotter it is, the quicker it is (reds tend to ferment at higher temperatures to extract flavour and colour from the skins); if it's cooler, it takes longer (more common for whites, to protect the subtle, delicate fragrances). As a rule, it's usually two to four weeks.

Much of this takes place in big stainless-steel tanks, particularly for everyday still whites. Sometimes it's in big wooden vats, sometimes in lined concrete. Occasionally wines are fermented in small oak barrels called barriques. This draws out interesting flavours from the wood and helps develop the wine's existing flavours.

FERMENTATION STOPS WHEN

A there's no sugar left, so the yeast dies

B the yeast drowns in its own effluent (alcohol)

C SO_2 is added to kill the yeast

D the pressure gets too high and kills the yeast

E the temperature drops too low and the yeast stops working

F the yeast is filtered out

After fermentation, there's a pile of sludge at the bottom of the fermentation vessel made up of dead yeast cells and various bits of skin, stalk and grape. This is called the lees. If wine is left in contact with this gunk (which is a more common practice in white wines than reds), it can lead to a wine with fuller flavour and texture. Muscadet, for example, a dry white from the Loire region, is sometimes made as plain 'Muscadet', but sometimes as 'Muscadet *sur lie*' – French for 'on the lees'. The latter wine has more flavour.

Before bottling, there are two more optional treatments: *fining and filtration.*

In the past, winemakers used animal products such as egg white, ox blood or fish bladders as fining (or clarifying) agents. Ox blood is now illegal since the BSE scare of the 1990s, while isinglass (ground fish bladders) is rarely used. These days, a type of earth called bentonite and man-made chemicals are the most common fining agents that are employed by winemakers.

Once a wine finishes fermenting, it can contain natural substances that make it cloudy. Fining gets rid of this haziness, which is often caused by 'colloids': small molecules, often of old grape matter. Though too small to be filtered, they have a positive electric charge. Since opposites attract, colloids avoid each other while suspended in wine. Fining is accomplished by adding negatively charged colloids. The particles then clump together, making them big enough either to filter out or else drop to the bottom, and the wine can then be drawn (or 'racked') off. A winemaker may also filter a wine to remove any sediment, or to get rid of yeast that may start to ferment again later.

Neither fining nor filtration is necessary, and if you're not careful, you may actually remove flavour components that make good wines delicious. Some people don't like finding 'bits' in the bottom of their bottles, which is fair enough, but it is the sign of a brave winemaker – one who cares more about the wine's flavour than anything else.

NATURAL WINES It's possible to go *au naturel* when winemaking. Minimal manipulation of the juice, no added acidity or sugar, minimal SO_2, no fining or filtration, and organic or biodynamic methods using natural yeasts are the main tenets of the movement towards 'natural wines'. There is no precise definition of what a 'natural wine' is, and no certifying body, which leads to disagreement as to its meaning. What is certain is that this growing group of (mostly French and Italian) small-scale winemakers is making interesting stuff, much of which is on the wilder fringes of winemaking.

Aging in oak

Once fermentation is complete, Many wines go straight into bottles and onto shelves, especially whites. Some, however, are aged first in tanks, wooden casks or simply in bottle. Usually only wines with strong flavours can handle wood-aging, and they are aged in barrels for a number of reasons. First, while watertight, wood isn't airtight, so oxygen seeps in through its pores; this subtly affects the wine, helping it to mature. Second, aging adds complexity, usually in the form of a slightly sweet vanilla flavour from a natural oak compound called vanillin. It can also add a touch of smoke. Finally, wood tannins from barrels pass into the wine, adding to any tannins extracted from the grapes.

Oak type is important. French oak (used in Bordeaux) is more subtle, whereas American oak (used in Rioja) adds a stronger flavour. Oak from France's Limousin region imparts lots of tannin, while trees from the Tronçais region provide less. Barrel-age is also a factor. New barrels give off more flavour and tannin than old ones, so a wine must be full-flavoured to start with if it's to cope with these. New wood also ages wine quicker, because wood pores get blocked with age. Other variables are the degree of 'toast' (flaming the inside of a barrel before wine is added), barrel size, cellar temperature, etc. On average, wine spends between six months in old wood for a light effect, and up to two years for others, such as intensely flavoured sweet wines. In fortified wines such as Madeira, wine stays in wood for decades. But oak barrels are expensive, so winemakers have other ways of getting similar effects: adding oak staves, oak chips, oak 'tea-bags' or oak essence (yuck).

Aging in bottles

Aging wine in barrels is an aerobic process (i.e. involving oxygen), whereas aging in bottle is mainly anaerobic (without oxygen). Over time, various constituents (acid, alcohol, tannin, flavour compounds, water) react with each other and add to a wine's flavour. If a bottle is closed with a cork, this lets in a tiny amount of air, which helps mature the wine, allowing more complex flavours to develop. Even modern screwcaps allow a miniscule degree of oxygen exchange. Some wines get better the older they become, since these reactions continue over time. But usually only wines with powerful flavours and a good level of acidity (and tannin if red) have the strength to improve in bottle.

I n this chapter we'll look at some practical approaches to tasting wine and some useful things to consider while you're drinking it. We'll also look at how to tell if a wine is faulty.

The best way to taste wines is in company, such as tasting wine with friends. It's more fun when a few of you are together and you can talk about what you're getting from each wine. For instance, I have a handful of really nice bottles in my 'cellar' at home (i.e. the bottom of the wardrobe). Much as I love to crack open a bottle while watching a DVD after work, I just can't bring myself to open my most exciting ones without having friends around and getting the chance to talk about the wines; otherwise, it feels like a missed opportunity. So much about wine-drinking is sharing, whether it be the wine in the bottle, the laughs during the evening, the dancing or the lazy Sunday on the sofa with the papers the day after.

By 'in company' I also mean opening more than one bottle at a time. Opening a bottle by itself is fine, but to get the most out of tasting, thinking about and talking about wine, it's better to have several bottles to compare and contrast. It's easier to get a complete impression of a wine when it's joined by others. You can always open one Sauvignon Blanc from New Zealand today and another tomorrow, then try to compare them from memory, but details are much clearer when both are in front of you at the same time. And if you've a few bottles open, so much the better: that's when you really notice the nuances and recognize common qualities in varieties, regions, producers, even vintages. Just remember: when tasting more than one bottle at a time, it's worth thinking about what order to drink them in.

1 **TYPE** Start with sparkling, then move on to whites, then reds, then sweet wines. The dissolved sugar in sweet wines can coat the mouth and make it more difficult to taste other things afterwards.

2 **FLAVOUR INTENSITY** Start with the lightest in flavour, then move towards the strongest in flavour.

3 **QUALITY** Start with the lowest quality level, then move towards the highest.

4 **AGE** I start with the youngest, moving towards the oldest to get a sense of progression and development. Some tackle this the other way around because flavours are more subtle and delicate in older wines and can take more concentration. At the end of the day, though, the best order to drink them in is just the order you feel like.

glug
glug
GLUG

How to taste wine

Every physical sense is indulged when you're drinking a glass of wine. Even before the wine is out of the bottle, you hear the joyful sound of the cork popping out, followed by the greedy *glug-glug-glugging* as the wine is being poured. You never know precisely what colour you'll see until it settles in your glass and you can see the gradations of different shades, from the core of the liquid to the paler edge where it touches the sides. The feel of wine in the mouth is uniquely pleasurable: there's the acidity on your tongue, the tannins on your gums, the refreshment of a chilled white, the warmth of a red, not to mention the way it slides across the mouth. And all this even before taste, the most indulged of all the senses, comes into play. But the sensual side of wine is just one reason for opening a bottle.

Wine doesn't just affect the body; it also has a unique and wonderful effect on the mind and spirit.

Primarily, though, wine tasting involves concentrating on the flavours and tastes that the glass of wine offers you. It's not that different to how you taste orange juice. You just give it a bit more attention, because many of the smells and tastes are subtle and fleeting, and a good glass of wine can have several different discernible aromas and flavours to enjoy – rather than just 'oranges'.

The most important thing to remember is simply to take your time at every stage.

TASTING –
the mouth

The tongue picks up only five different taste sensations: sweetness, acidity, bitterness, saltiness and umami. In case you're unfamiliar with umami, it is Japanese for 'deliciousness', but it's what we might call a kind of meaty savouriness; it is found in high concentration in meats such as beef and pork, in shellfish and seafood like prawns, scallops, tuna and mackerel, in mushrooms, soy sauce, some cheeses, etc. Although not typically found in wine, umami is a factor when it comes to food and wine matching, which we'll look at later on.

When tasting wine, start to think about the intensity of each of the following components, from a lot to a little of each.

Sweetness

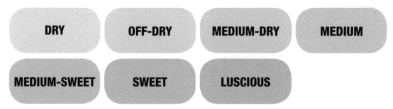

The vast majority of all table wine, whether red, white or rosé is dry.

Acidity

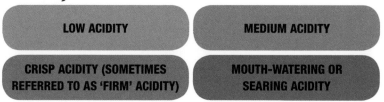

All wines have acidity. It is one of their most important characteristics and it's what makes them refreshing. It is important to get the level correct, though – i.e. in balance with other components of the wine.

Tannins

LOW TANNINS   MEDIUM TANNINS   STRONG TANNINS

Mysterious stuff, tannin. It's a naturally occurring group of compounds found in some fruits and vegetables, but it itself is tasteless. Rather than taste, it gives a sensation: a kind of drying, gripping impression that makes your tongue feel like it's sticking to the roof of your mouth. You get it in strong tea and rhubarb as well as wine. When it comes to wine, though, tannin comes from the stalks, pips and skins of the grape, so there is almost always some level of tannin in red wines. You also get it in oak barrels (wood tannins), and it leaches out into the wines, which is why you might also get a little tannin in oak-aged whites such as top Burgundies, top Chablis or traditional white Rioja, for example. Tannins have different discernible textures in the mouth that range from powdery to rough to smooth to grainy; they can also be bitter or soft or ripe or chewy.

Body

LIGHT BODY   MEDIUM BODY   FULL BODY   HEAVY

Compared to water, wine usually feels thicker and more viscous when it's in the mouth. This is due mostly to wine's alcohol and dissolved sugar. So a wine is either full-bodied, medium-bodied or light-bodied. 'Full-bodied' is also sometimes used to describe wine when it is full of flavour/alcohol/body/tannin – i.e. a 'big' wine.

Alcohol

VERY LOW ALCOHOL   LOW ALCOHOL   MEDIUM ALCOHOL

HIGH ALCOHOL   VERY HIGH (HOT)

Most reds, whites and rosés are between 8.5% alcohol by volume (ABV) for the lightest German Riesling – to 15.5% ABV for the biggest California Zinfandel. Again, balance is key: high or low alcohol isn't a bad thing in itself unless a wine is out of balance.

So there's a limit to the number of sensations you can get from wine in your mouth. Various sensations are experienced in different parts of the mouth, which is why, when taking in a sip, it's best to roll it around the mouth, tongue and gums before you swallow so that you can get a proper impression of the wine as a whole, with all its elements.

But what about the other flavours, such as fruit flavours in wine? People talk about 'wine tasting', but the most pleasure when enjoying a glass of wine comes not from the mouth but from the nose. Imagine taking a sip of wine while holding your nose. See what I mean?

TASTING –
the nose

Smell

| LOW INTENSITY | MEDIUM INTENSITY | HIGH INTENSITY |

On one level, smell can also be judged on a sliding scale of intensity. But on another level, there are the *types* of aromas you get. This is where wine gets interesting and fun; you have to use your brain to identify what you're tasting.

The sense of smell is employed in two ways. First, you smell the wine in the glass before you've tasted it. Second, once you've taken a sip and rolled the wine around your mouth, you breathe through your nose. As you breathe, the wine evaporates up the back of your throat and into your nose.

If you've ever been to a wine tasting (or sat next to a geek like me at dinner), you might occasionally hear little slurping noises. This is because you can aid this evaporative tasting experience by sucking air through the wine in your mouth. If you purse your lips and suck air in through them while you've got a mouthful of wine at the front of your mouth, the air picks up flavours and they go up into your nose. If you haven't done it before, try it; it will be a revelation. You'll sound like you're gurgling in the bath (if you know what I mean), but, all of a sudden, you'll taste the wine in full Technicolor. Soon you'll be doing it after every other sip.

Just don't blame me if your friends think you're a weirdo.

To begin with, look for some simple fruit flavours. Almost all wines, particularly younger wines, will have some kind of fruit flavour: for example, raspberries, strawberries or blackcurrants in red wines; apples, peaches, kiwis, etc., in whites.

The more you try and pick out flavours, the better you get at it, so if you're picking up melon aromas, try to be more precise; ask yourself what type of melon – honeydew or watermelon, perhaps.

Sometimes the aroma will be more general and indistinct, but sometimes you can be more accurate: so don't just think of 'strawberry' flavours, but try to work out whether it's wild strawberry, tinned strawberry, or strawberry jam.

In addition to fruit, there are other types of aromas you'll find in wines. Herbs and spice scents are common, as are vegetal tones such as cabbage or asparagus. Meaty or animal aromas are also widespread, especially in older red wines. Dairy scents such as butter, yoghurt or cream are often present, especially in whites, as are floral notes. Try and be more accurate here as well. If you can detect a spicy smell, is it cinnamon, clove, nutmeg or something else?

Look for a range of top-level scents first; then, once you've identified these, you can drill down into a more precise definition of the particulars. On the opposite page is a list of possible aromas you could get, and how you might refine them to greater accuracy. This isn't a list of all the smells and tastes you could get from a bottle of wine, but it will serve as a framework to start you off.

Top Level	2nd Level		3rd Level	4th Level
1. Fruit	i.	Berry fruit	Blackcurrant, blackberry, redcurrant, raspberry, strawberry	Cooked? Fresh? Sweets? Tinned?
	ii.	Stone fruit	Apricot, peach	
	iii.	Tropical fruit	Guava, melon, pineapple	
	iv.	Orchard fruit	Apple, pear	
	v.	Citrus fruit	Orange, lemon, lime, grapefruit, kumquat	
2. Herb	i.	Woody	Rosemary, thyme	Powdered?
	ii.	Leafy	Basil, dill, sage, oregano, mint	Fresh?
3. Spice	i.	Sweet	Cinnamon, clove	
	ii.	Savoury	Black pepper	
	iii.	Aromatic	Star anise	
4. Mineral	i.	Hot bricks		
	ii.	Flint		
	iii.	Chalk	in rock, dust	
5. Animal	i.	Cooked meat	Lamb, beef, chicken, game	
	ii.	Raw meat	Beef, chicken, game	
	iii.	Animal hide	Leather, dog's coat, wool	
	iv.	Manure	Chicken, cow, human	
6. Chemical	i.	Sulphur		
	ii.	Iodine		
	iii.	Petrol		
7. Dairy	i.	Yoghurt		
	ii.	Cream		
	iii.	Butter		
	iv.	Cheese	Blue, hard, soft	
	v.	Milk	Fresh, spoiled	
8. Vegetal	i.	Cabbage	Fresh, boiled	
	ii.	Asparagus	Fresh, tinned	
	iii.	Peas	Fresh pods, tins	
9. Woodland	i.	Truffle	Black, white	Cooked?
	ii.	Forest floor		Raw?
	iii.	Mushroom		Mouldy?
	iv.	Moss		Wet?
	v.	Bark		Dry?
	vi.	Pine		

COMMON GRAPE VARIETIES AND
their typical tastes/smells

Reds

Cabernet Sauvignon – Cassis, pencil shavings, tobacco, green pepper

Merlot – Plum, prunes, blackberry

Pinot Noir – Strawberry, raspberry, beetroot, mushroom, farmyard aromas

Cabernet Franc – Blackcurrant, blackcurrant bush, pencil lead, raspberry

Gamay – Cherry, strawberry, raspberry, banana

Malbec – Blackberry, violets, meat

Mourvèdre – Blackberries, damsons, prunes, compost, violets

Grenache/Garnacha – Strawberry, mocha, dried herbs, plums

Shiraz/Syrah – Black fruits, black pepper, bacon, smoke

Nebbiolo – Roses, tar, cherries, liquorice, star anise, truffle

Sangiovese – Cherry, violets, almonds

Tempranillo – Roses, leather, red and black fruits, tea

Carmenère – Blackberry, blackcurrant, tomato stalk, red bell pepper

Zinfandel – Liquorice, spice, blackcurrant, wild red berries, dark chocolate

Pinotage – Strawberry, damson, nail varnish, sweet spices, meat

Carignan – Bramble, animals, dried figs

Cinsaut/Cinsault – Red fruits, plums, floral

Whites

Chardonnay – Apples, pears, peaches, citrus fruit, melon, pineapple, dairy

Sauvignon Blanc – Gooseberry, kiwi, elderflower, asparagus, cut grass

Chenin Blanc/Steen – Quince, lemon, wet dog, honey

Pinot Gris/Pinot Grigio – Apple, pear, melon, Turkish delight

Muscat – Fresh green grapes, floral

Pinot Blanc – Apple, peach, yellow fruits

Sémillon – Lime, satsuma, wax

Marsanne – Celery, apricot, peach, rhubarb, mango

Roussanne – Peach, musk

Viognier – White peach, apricot, floral

Malvasia – Pear, melon, apricot

Ugni Blanc/Trebbiano – Faintly of melon and almonds... not much

Riesling – Lemon and lime, petrol, satsuma, jasmine

Gewürztraminer – Turkish delight, rose, lychee, cinnamon, soap

Sylvaner – Apples, floral, earth

Verdelho – Peach, apricot, greengage, limey citrus fruit

Torrontés – Apricot, peach, green grapes, faintly spicy, floral

Grüner Veltliner – Peach, green apple, white pepper

Albariño – Green apple, honeysuckle, lemon, jasmine, peach

WINE *faults*

A few other potential smells can be found in wine if it is faulty – and these are less welcome. A number of things can go wrong with a bottle of wine. On the whole, bad bottles aren't that common these days, because technology has improved, and wineries, even in poorer countries, have become cleaner and more modern. Annoyingly, though, faults do occur more frequently in very old – and therefore more expensive – bottles. This is often due to inadequate storage, or to the fact that wineries weren't run as well many years ago as they are today.

Corked wine

The most common wine fault is when a bottle is 'corked'. This happens when a chemical called trichloroanisole (TCA), which is sometimes found in natural cork, taints the wine in the bottle. Some people say that as many as one in ten bottles are affected, but up to one in 30 is probably a more accurate guess.

You can tell if a wine's corked from the way it smells and tastes; sometimes it's obvious that something is wrong, but sometimes it's more subtle – from a little bit corked to a lot. When it's strong, the smell is like wet cardboard, mushrooms or a dank basement. Sometimes, however, it's just a feeling that the taste of the wine is somehow muted, and you're just not getting much pleasure from drinking it.

If you come across a wine that is corked, simply put the cork back in the bottle, take it back to where you got it and they should give you a refund. Shops tend to claim the money back from the shipper or distributor, and then they tend to claim at least some of that money back from the producer. This is the major benefit of screwcaps: no more corked wine.

Sometimes if you open a bottle you might get little bits of cork swimming around in the wine. This doesn't mean it's 'corked', though, so just fish them out with your finger. They don't do any harm to anyone.

Many wines are fermented in big stainless-steel tanks, particularly everyday still whites. Sometimes fermentation takes place in big wooden vats, or painted concrete ones (not a bad thing). Occasionally wines (mainly expensive ones) are fermented in small oak barrels known as barriques. This draws out interesting flavours from the wood and helps mature and develop existing flavours.

Oxidized wine

Another problem with the occasional bottle is that the wine has become oxidized. If a cork or screwcap doesn't fit properly and lets air into the bottle, the wine can be spoiled. You'll know because it will smell and taste dull and lifeless, without any fresh, fruity aromas, and sometimes with a hint of sherry about it. If it's a white wine, often the colour will be a touch brown around the edges. If this is coupled with a burned, caramelized flavour, then it suggests that the bottle has been stored at too high a temperature, and the wine is described as tasting 'madeirized'. Again, this is quite unusual, but if it happens, simply send or take the bottle back.

Other wine faults and deposits

Once upon a time, if a wine was cloudy, it would always have been sent back, because this can be a fault caused by certain bacteria. It still is a fault for most wines, but for some natural wines that aren't fined or filtered, cloudiness is now an accepted feature. This should be pointed out to you when you buy it, though, and admittedly it's still pretty unusual.

Some faults in a wine can be detected by the eye before the glass gets under your nose.

Sometimes you also get a deposit in red wines, and this is caused by the tannins and other compounds in the wine sticking together and dropping out of suspension. This isn't a fault as such – just a natural part of the aging process. Either decant the wine or just pour it carefully; otherwise the last sip might be a bit, erm, crunchy.

Another common type of deposit, particularly in white wines, consists of small crystals either stuck to the underside of the cork or sitting at the bottom of the bottle. Although they can look disturbingly like tiny shards of glass, they are usually just potassium bitartrate crystals. These form naturally if the wine gets very cold, but they are nothing to worry about and don't affect a wine's flavour. Some wineries super-chill their wines to filter out any potential crystals before bottling, but others prefer not to manipulate wine in this way. Again, just pour the wine carefully and leave them resting in the bottom of the bottle.

3

TALKING
ABOUT
WINE

without
FEELING
AWKWARD

he nose and mouth can sometimes be a little vague in the way they try and tell us what they're sensing. Smell and taste are not as powerful or precise in their function as sight or touch. So it helps to talk about what you are smelling or tasting. Sometimes you can't quite put your finger on a particular smell, or don't even notice one that is staring you in the face until someone mentions it. People often suspect that a lot of bullshit is talked about wine. I've encountered some hilarious descriptions of wines when marketing departments have strayed from describing actual flavours into the realms of poetic whimsy. But most of the time, it's not what is said that's the problem, just the *way* it is said.

WHY WINE-TALK MAKES PEOPLE
feel uncomfortable

1 Eccentric wine commentators

For some reason, wine has had more than its fair share of wacky commentators over the years, but you really don't have to wear a monocle and bark in rhyming couplets to talk about it. A British critic still invoked today starred on a 1980s-90s BBC TV show called *Food and Drink*. It was a great show that helped make food and wine more accessible for a lot of people, but a presenter called Jilly Goolden offered some ebullient, vivid and occasionally baffling descriptions of what she tasted. Few, if any, other programmes at the time featured wine, so it was many people's only experience of hearing anyone talk about it. Goolden's slightly bizarre delivery and descriptions frightened some people away, yet she's not the world's only wine eccentric. I suppose a glass of red liquid on a TV screen isn't that interesting without someone trying to convey the aromas and flavours that make it special. But don't worry: talking about wine *doesn't* make you batty. That's all in the delivery. And the bow ties.

2 It's a bit 'posh'

Wine is sometimes considered one of the last bastions of the middle and upper classes. This is a pretty outdated point of view. Truth is, most wine is bought at the supermarket during the weekly shopping expedition alongside the baked beans and toilet roll – not brought up from the cellar by Jeeves to accompany truffled swan. Fifty years ago, all food or drink shipped over from abroad was a luxury, but nowadays a bottle of great wine needn't cost any more than a night down the pub. Wine is something for everyone to enjoy; those who think it's elitist should spend a night on the town with some Australian winemakers.

3 Not knowing which terms to use

For most wine drunk on a day-to-day basis, we only need to use fairly simple terms. Is it sweet or dry? Is it high in acidity? Does it have a lot of tannin? Can you detect any oak flavours? What other flavours do you taste: just fruit flavours, or others like nuts, herbs, spices?

To begin with, when trying to identify particular elements, it can feel odd saying you taste apples, pears and melons in a glass of wine; after all, it's made of grapes. But when it ages in bottle or barrel, the various constituents in a wine react with each other, creating new flavour compounds that can be exactly the same as those found in other plants or foods. So, when you're tasting a wine and you can taste strawberries, it may not be the case that the wine simply tastes *like* strawberries; in all likelihood you're tasting the very same flavour compound actually found in a strawberry. So, if you ever feel self-conscious or silly naming some of the various flavours you're getting – don't. Chances are, you are actually tasting them.

When drawing conclusions about wine, think BLIC: *Balance, Length, Intensity, Complexity*. What's the overall balance of all the wine's elements? How long does the flavour linger in the mouth? How intense are the flavours and aromas? And how many identifiable aromas and flavours can you find – i.e. how complex is it? These are the criteria to think about when judging wine quality.

4 'Getting it wrong'

Some people avoid talking about wine for fear of 'getting it wrong'. We've all tasted hundreds of different flavours in different foods and drinks, and we trust our palates normally. Wine is no different, and there's no reason to doubt our sense of taste. Making a judgment about the sugar, acidity or alcohol levels in a wine is no more difficult than judging the salt, vinegar or greasiness levels in a bag of chips. It's a myth that you need some kind of special abilities to be able to taste and enjoy wine. If you have a nose and a mouth, there's no reason you can't enjoy it just as much as anyone else.

As for using the 'wrong' word to describe a wine, stick to natural flavours and you'll be fine. Name any fruit, vegetable, herb, spice or animal product and there'll be a wine out there somewhere that contains that flavour. Sometimes it's fun to use random words, but if you're really trying to communicate, it's easier to compare flavours and aromas to other types of food or drink. And as for judging quality levels, don't forget that it's just a matter of taste. When all is said and done, it's not easy to buy a genuinely dreadful wine these days. Once in a while you might get a bottle that isn't exactly what you expected, but that's all part of the fun.

WINE TASTING
glossary

Below are some terms you might hear at a wine tasting and what they mean. Instead of alphabetical order, they're listed in the order you normally experience a wine: how it looks, smells and tastes, along with terms that relate to evaluating it.

How it looks

Appearance There are several things to take into account here: colour, brightness, clarity, bubbles.

Rim/core The colour of the outer rim of the wine in a glass compared to its colour in the centre. Tip the glass on its side in front of a white background (a piece of paper is fine). In a white wine, any green hints mean it's likely to be young; if it's golden, it's probably older. With a red, if there are bright-purple tints it's likely to be young; brick-red and it's probably more mature.

Bead If it's sparkling, the bubbles tend to rise in little lines. This is the 'bead' – like beads on a necklace. The smaller the bubbles, the softer the 'mousse'.

How it smells

Nose The smell of a wine. Sometimes used as a verb: to 'nose' a glass of wine.

Unclean/Dirty There's something amiss. The wine smells wrong, like you wouldn't really want to drink it, or you wouldn't get much pleasure if you did.

Bouquet The collection of aromas the wine produces, particularly with reference to tertiary aromas from aging (this term is a bit old-fashioned).

Primary flavours/aromas A grape variety's basic fruit flavours and aromas in a young wine, like raspberry/strawberry in Pinot Noir, blackcurrant/green bell pepper in Cabernet Sauvignon, apple/melon in Chardonnay, etc.

Secondary flavours/aromas These come from the winemaking process, such as vanilla and smoke from the use of oak barrels.

Tertiary flavours/aromas Those that occur after a wine has matured, like leather, meat, wood and spice; even 'farmyard' or 'barnyard' aromas, i.e. in a 'countryside' way rather than a nasty, 'open sewer' way. The latter would be 'dirty'.

Youthful Still has lots of primary aromas. 'Young' means 'made recently' – two years might make it 'youthful' if it's a big red meant for aging, but it might be 'mature' if it's a white made to be drunk young.

Mature Ready to drink, possibly displaying some tertiary aromas. Might be a one-year-old white wine or a 30-year-old bottle of Port.

Closed A wine that isn't giving off much smell. This might be because it's still very young, or because it's just going through an awkward phase.

Developed Showing some tertiary aromas; showing some age.

How it tastes – evaluation

Palate Your tasting apparatus: tongue, gums, lips, throat, even teeth.

Dry The opposite of sweet. 'Bone-dry' is a wine with no hint of sweetness.

Flabby/Blowsy If acidity is too low and unbalanced, the wine is 'flabby'.

Racy/Nervy Noticeable but balanced acidity.

Mouth-watering Used when acidity is high – not necessarily a bad thing.

Warm/Hot If the alcohol level is too high; has a warm sensation on the finish.

Mousse The fizziness in sparkling wines. It might be harsh and aggressive like in a can of cola, or delicate, like in good-quality sparkling wines.

Green The wine tastes like it was made from grapes that weren't fully ripe.

Fleshy A wine with lots of ripe fruit flavours and at least medium body.

Austere The acidity and/or tannin are more obvious than the fruit.

Spritz Or 'prickle'. When a wine isn't fully sparkling, but has a fizzy sensation.

Minerality Used mainly to describe an aroma of wet stones, flint or chalk.

Structure Refers to acidity and tannins, rather than flavours.

Complex In the most remarkable wines there are many – perhaps a dozen or more – different discernible aromas. These make it 'complex'.

Balance The balance of flavour components: tannin, acidity, sweetness, alcohol, intensity of flavour, etc. Ideally, all elements need to be in balance.

Finish The flavours and sensations that remain just as/after you swallow.

Long When the taste lingers. Long is good if it's a nice taste.

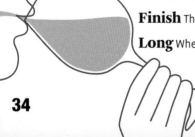

BLAGGING
it

At certain times you need to look like you know what you're doing: at a wine tasting, for example, or if you're going on a date with someone who's really into wine. Here are a few things to remember to make you look like a pro.

1 **ONLY FILL A WINE GLASS A THIRD OF THE WAY UP.** This gives you room to swirl it around the glass before you take a sip – without getting it all over your companion's shirt/dress.

2 **SWIRL THE WINE AROUND THE GLASS BEFORE YOU TAKE A SIP!** Don't just dive in, take a slurp, gulp it down and go 'aaaah!'. First, look at the wine to gauge its colour. Then take a sniff to see what it smells like. Only then take a sip.

3 **PAUSE BRIEFLY AFTER YOU'VE SWALLOWED** to make you look like you're thinking about what you've just tasted.

4 **NOW SAY ONE OF THE FOLLOWING:**
- If it's a recent vintage: 'Quite developed for a young wine.'
- If it's an older bottle: 'Lovely developed aromas coming through.'
- If it's a red: 'Interesting tannins.'
- If it's a white: 'Good minerality.'
- If it's from the New World (i.e. not Europe): 'Clearly New World; lovely, vibrant fruit.'
- If it's from the Old World (e.g. France, Spain, Italy, Portugal or Germany): 'Beautiful Old World character; not too obvious.'

5 **CHUCK IN A FEW OF THE WORDS** listed in the glossary and you're golden.

6 **NOW CHANGE THE SUBJECT – FAST.** Or read the rest of this book.

4

BUYING WINE: SAFE BETS, what TO AVOID AND where TO GET THE GOOD STUFF!

• You know exactly what the wine is for (drink/dinner with friends/gift).

• You know exactly who's going to drink it and the kind of thing they like.

• If having food, you know exactly what you're going to eat with it.

• You have all the time in the world to think about what would work.

• You're at a computer so you can search the internet for shops.

• You have your phone on you to call them to check it's in stock.

• You have a chauffeur-driven limo waiting to take you to the shop to buy it, then take you home.

IN PRACTICE...

• You're on the way to your friends' house for dinner.

• You've no idea what you're going to eat.

• You're not sure what they like.

• You're late, so you have to pick up something on the way.

Or

• It's a friend's birthday, you don't have a gift and need a bottle for a present.

• You're not sure what they like.

• You're late, so you have to pick up something on the way.

Or

• You're going to your girlfriend/boyfriend's parents' place for the first time.

• You're not sure what they like.

• You're late, so you have to pick up something on the way.

We all find ourselves in this position from time to time. If it's a gift and you don't know what people will like, choose a reliable crowd-pleaser (see 'Good Bets', page 40).

If it's dinner and you don't know what people will be eating, go for something medium-weight and versatile, such as unoaked Chardonnay, white or red Côtes du Rhône, red or white Burgundy, red Rioja, Pinot Gris, medium-bodied reds or whites from New Zealand; anything from Western Australia; French *vins de pays*/IGPs (see page 75), Pinot Noir. Avoid Sauvignon Blanc: it can clash with richer dishes.

But where to get it?

The chances of walking by a quality wine shop are almost nil. This leaves three choices (depending on where you live), all of which call for different strategies:

- Corner shop/convenience store/petrol station
- Supermarket
- Wine-shop chain

In the UK, the corner shop or convenience store is one of those rare cases when it's best to stick to big brands, because inevitably there'll be a load of French, Spanish and Italian wines you've never heard of on the shelves, and chances are they'll be pretty shabby. A few rules of thumb:

- Choose a recognizable big brand, since this stock turns over quickly. Go for the best you can find; country of origin doesn't really matter.
- Accept that you'll pay £2 more than in the supermarket or online. That's life.
- Does it have dust on it? Avoid.
- Is it more than five years old? Avoid.
- If you see a) Torres b) Marqués de Cáceres c) Concha y Toro, you're sorted. If not, go for Jacob's Creek or Robert Mondavi. Safe is better than bad.

Supermarkets are trickier. Some have decent ranges, some don't. Rules of thumb:

- Check out the offers, but don't be a promotions junkie; they're not always the best bet and you rarely get anything that interesting offered '3 for 2'.
- Don't rule out the supermarket's 'finest' own-label range. These are sometimes good quality and value.
- Supermarket 'fine wine' selections can be a source of quality at a good price.

In some US states, the lack of the supermarket option has led to an increase in independent wine shops, which has worked out favourably for consumers.

Small wine-shop chains have better buying power than individual stores, so their prices can be good, though sometimes with less specialist ranges. Rules of thumb:

- There's more scope to be adventurous and end up with something decent here than in the corner shop or the supermarket.

- It can be worth asking the staff for recommendations.

- Check out single-bottle promotions, but you might get better value from more unusual wines than big brands or famous regional names.

Keeping a few bottles at home ensures you'll have a decent one when you need it. Of course, you can get good wines from off-licence chains or supermarkets, but they're rarely a consistent source of the best. For the most joyful bottles, go to an independent wine merchant, either physically or online. Most sizeable towns have at least one; a quick search on the net should help you find yours.

Ironically, in wine-producing countries it can be difficult to get good wine from other countries, but the internet is very helpful. Check out websites like www.wine-searcher.com.

Independent wine merchants have advantages over supermarkets and chains.

- They tend to be run by people who have a passion for wine, so they'll go to great lengths to get hold of a few cases of well-made, exciting bottles.

- Many fine wines come from small, family-owned estates with artisan winemakers who make small amounts of wine – too small for supermarkets to bother with. And some estates (especially in Burgundy) only deal with independent wine merchants who've represented them for years.

- They can stock wines from unusual grape varieties or regions that might be overlooked elsewhere, selling them to regular customers on recommendation.

What supermarkets and big chains do have on the little guys is buying power, and buyers willing to negotiate hard in price terms. These factors equate to lower prices, and there's no way the little guys can compete. But they can get a lot of brilliant wines the big guys can't get their hands on. The added bonus of shopping at your local wine shop is service: someone who can tell you all about a wine, make suggestions, and possibly give you ideas on food and wine matching. And finally, the money you spend in independent shops is more likely to stay in your local community.

✔ **WINES THAT ARE TYPICALLY GOOD BETS IF YOU DON'T WANT TO SPEND MUCH**
- Chile, especially Chilean Cabernet Sauvignon
- Argentina, especially Malbec and Torrontés
- Navarra (Spain), especially reds
- Portugal
- Southern Italy
- Languedoc-Roussillon (France)
- Loire (France), not including Sancerre
- Rueda (Spain)
- Verdicchio (Italy)
- Sparkling? Look to Spain (Cava), Italy (Prosecco), New Zealand, Tasmania, Australia, Loire

✔ **EXPLORE: UNUSUAL WINES THAT CAN BE SUPERB (AND OFTEN GOOD VALUE)**
- German whites and reds
- Sherry
- Madeira
- Vouvray (France)
- Gewürztraminer

✘ **REGIONS TO AVOID IF YOU DON'T HAVE MUCH CASH**
- Bordeaux, including Sauternes (France)
- Burgundy (France)
- Chablis (France)
- Sancerre (France)
- Barolo (Italy)
- Barbaresco (Italy)
- Champagne
- California
- Châteauneuf-du Pape (France)

But, if you do have at least £20 to spend, this is often where the real classics are to be found.

✘ **BETTER AVOIDED ON THE WHOLE**
- New World White Grenache
- White Zinfandel
- Portuguese rosés
- Shiraz rosés
- Anything that says 'blush' on the label
- Ruby Cabernet
- Most Pinot Grigio
- Anything with a novelty label or bottle
- Cream or pale cream Sherry

A friend once said to me that he never felt sure if he could trust independent wine shops – that they might try to rip him off because they could tell he didn't know much about wine. I can't vouch for them all, but the majority of the ones I know are in it for love, not money. If you're uncertain about what to buy, particularly if you want something special, they're an invaluable source of advice.

VERY EXPENSIVE
bottles

Not all wines are worth discussing in depth. If you're chilling on the couch with a bottle of cheap Aussie Shiraz on a Monday night, you probably don't want to analyse the tannins; you just want something soothing in your tummy. If it's your birthday, wedding anniversary or you've just won some money on the horses, then you might want a more interesting bottle. If it costs more than £8 in the shops, or more than £20 in a restaurant, it should at least be interesting enough for you to stop and have a quick think about what you're drinking.

In theory, the more you pay, the more time it's worth spending. Wine only starts getting interesting from around £7 a bottle in shops, but this is far from all of them. Once you get to £10 a bottle, it should be interesting on some level no matter what it is (apart from sparkling wines, Ports and the like, which are more expensive to produce). The real value is between £12 and £30. Certain wines, such as Burgundy and Bordeaux, are only worth buying in this cost bracket. If you're buying a bottle at this price level, it should be worth remembering and a real pleasure to drink. If it's not, something's either wrong with the bottle – or the place you bought it.

But what about the other end of the list? The sexy end with the four-digit prices? What makes these so special? Three factors: fashion, quality and scarcity. Each of these can make a wine expensive. Two will make it extremely expensive. Rarely do all three come together at the same time, but, if the quality's extremely high and hardly any of it is made, then, like diamonds, it never goes out of fashion.

A certain level of quality in wine is vital. And it's largely true to say this is what makes a particular wine expensive; scarcity only sends the price up further. Just because a wine costs £1,000 a bottle doesn't mean it will send you into raptures; it probably means it's just really, really good wine: complex, long, balanced... an excellent example of its type by a top producer in an excellent year. If you're lucky, it'll knock your socks off, but price doesn't guarantee an unforgettable bottle. When it comes to wine, the law of diminishing returns is ever-present: the difference between a £4 bottle and a £5 bottle is huge; the difference between a £250 bottle and a £251 bottle is negligible.

The most expensive bottle sold to date was a Bordeaux: a bottle of 1947 Château Cheval Blanc for $304,375 (£192,000) at an auction in Geneva in 2010. Thankfully, only a very small percentage get above £100 per bottle in the shops. Often the more expensive ones are bought and sold by fine-wine brokers and opportunists who buy and sell speculatively to make a quick buck – not appreciate the wine.

5

IT IS
red WINE
WITH OSTRICH,
ISN'T IT...?

A lot is made of which wines should go with which foods. This is an area where people get unnerved, especially in restaurants: hence the invention of the sommelier (aka the wine waiter). This had the effect of unnerving people even more. It's actually all pretty straightforward, and there are a few rules of thumb that will help you make a reliable selection without too much effort.

In many European countries, people simply don't drink wine without food. The latter is a practice developed by barbarian booze hounds like the British. Drinking wine without eating can have pretty disastrous effects. Like falling on your bottom, leaving a party without telling anyone, getting in a cab and being unable to remember your own address. Or so I'm told. Yet most wines (in the Old World at least) have developed over centuries hand in hand with local cuisine; together, one shows off the other in its best light. So the traditional wines and cuisines of France, Italy, and Spain, evolved together as two sides of the same coin. While a plate of food is just dinner and a glass of wine alone can be a lovely drink, combine the two and you have a well-rounded meal that both quenches your thirst and sates your hunger. Most importantly, certain elements in specific wines bring out certain elements in specific foods – they become more than the sum of their parts. The wine also has the beneficial effect of 'cleansing your palate': mopping up the flavours of the previous mouthful, readying your mouth for the next bite.

Alcohol is blamed for so many ills, but alcoholic drinks are a wonderful blessing. Fermentation is a simple and often spontaneous biological process that occurs in the natural world. It supplies us with a clean, untreated, organic drink free from harmful bacteria thanks to the purifying alcohol, with multifarious health benefits. It creates previously undiscovered, unimagined aromas and flavours that can change, evolve and last indefinitely. And they go perfectly with dinner.

THE BASICS OF
food and wine matching

Still, food and wine matching is a bit of a black art. There is no simple three-point rule that will always get you to the 'right' bottle. How could there be, with all the ingredients, cooking methods and traditions that exist? Yet that's precisely what makes food and wine matching fun. Thankfully, there are a number of approaches you can use, and one golden rule:

The flavour of the wine should not be more or less powerful than the flavour of the food.

That is the most important thing to bear in mind, not colour. So if the food has a subtle flavour, go for a wine with a subtle flavour. If the food has big, powerful flavours, go for a big, powerful wine. If you're having grilled sole or a cold vegetable tart, pair it with a light wine, such as a Muscadet, a Chablis or a Beaujolais-Villages. Opt for venison stew or grilled T-bone steak, and you might want to try a big Californian Zinfandel, or a young Languedoc red. If you had the Zin with the vegetable tart, you wouldn't taste much of the subtlety of each vegetable, and the wine would just get in the way like a big, brutish bruiser. Pair the Chablis with the venison stew and you'd lose the delicate flavours of the wine and register acidity, turning a beautiful bottle into something a bit sour and resentful.

In addition, though, consider the dish's most prominent flavours:

Acidic
If your dish is sharp or sour, containing citrus juice or vinegar, choose an equally acidic wine, such as Loire Sauvignon, Albariño, Verdicchio, Chablis and Riesling for whites; Barbera, Valpolicella, Dornfelder and Bourgogne Pinot Noir for reds.

Sweet
If your dish has a hint of sweetness, such as a curry with fruit, or meat with a fruit sauce, choose a wine with a complementing hint of sweetness or ripe fruitiness, such as a Vouvray, Viognier, California Pinot Noir or Chilean Merlot.

Salty
If your dish has marked saltiness (some seafood dishes, for example), your best bets are often young, crisp, fresh whites without too much fruit: Muscadet, Chablis, Vinho Verde, etc. Another good alternative is fino or manzanilla Sherry.

Spicy
If your dish contains a lot of chilli, pepper or other heat-giving spice, avoid dry, subtle wines. Instead, try New World reds with lots of ripe, juicy fruit. If you fancy a white, go for something flavoursome but unoaked, like a Sauvignon Blanc or Torrontés. Off-dry whites, like some Rieslings and Gewürztraminers, can work extremely well.

Smoky
Smoked meats need something fairly gutsy. German Riesling (no sweeter than Spätlese) works well with smoked salmon or smoked eel; dry Riesling and Chenin Blanc are often good with smoked fish. For smoked poultry, try a peppery Syrah.

Savoury

Dishes high in umami (Parmesan, mushrooms, soy, seaweed, meat stocks) are best paired with medium- to full-bodied, complex reds. Barolo, Old World Pinot Noir, Châteauneuf-du-Pape and other Rhône reds can be good matches here. Amontillado or oloroso Sherries can be a better choice with foods like these.

Three other approaches that can be useful to bear in mind are harmony, contrast and quality.

Harmony

If particular flavours are found in a dish, find a wine that contains the same ones. For example, match a dish with earthy flavours to a wine with earthy flavours, and a dish with ripe, fruity flavours to a wine with ripe, fruity flavours.

Contrast

If one of the dish's primary characteristics is saltiness, you could try going for a sweet wine. If its defining characteristic is spiciness, opt for a very floral wine, and so on (big risk, but big reward with this approach).

Quality

Put simply, if you're having a fairly basic, everyday meal, go for a fairly basic, everyday wine. On the other hand, if you're going all out with some seriously complex and professional cooking, choose the best wine you can afford.

Additional points worth considering:

Hot or cold

If your meal is still sizzling, chances are you're going to want something with at least a medium level of flavour and richness.

If your meal was once cooked but is now cold, like cold cuts, quiche or certain types of sausage, opt for something less full.

If your meal never was cooked (i.e. you're eating it raw), chances are that you're eating either:

- raw veg, in which case your food/wine matching dedication should be applauded; try an Old World Sauvignon or a Bourgogne Aligoté

- raw meat e.g. carpaccio of beef – go for medium reds with good acidity: Chianti or Beaune or Beaujolais Cru, or even a medium- to full-bodied white

- raw fish, e.g. sushi and sashimi – go for sake, or fino or manzanilla Sherry, Chablis, or a dry sparkling wine

Cooking method

Certain types of cooking, particularly ones involving intense heat, can add intensity of flavour to a dish. So, if your food is poached in water, you might consider choosing a less powerful wine than if your food is fried. If your food is roasted, opt for something even fuller, and, if it's char-grilled, fuller still.

- Anything poached, even ham or chicken, will happily go with something as light as a medium-bodied white.

- Anything on the barbecue or grill will be able to handle a medium-bodied red at least, including fish.

Basically, the rule of thumb is: the longer and hotter the cooking method, the more intensely flavoured the finished dish will be. Result? The bigger and more powerful the wine you can match with it.

Seasoning, sauces and accompaniments

Don't forget to take all elements of a dish into account when considering a wine to go with it. Having lamb? Don't just think of a wine that goes with lamb; think about the sauce, the herbs or spices, and any other accompaniments.

If your dinner has a strongly flavoured sauce, give the sauce as much (if not more) thought as the thing it covers. If your steak has a pepper sauce, for instance, you'll want something more robust than if you were having it plain.

If your dinner is served plainly with some steamed veg, have something fairly light; if it's heavily spiced, look for something more robust. If you're having butternut squash soup with cream, you might want a white Burgundy (first considering the intensity of flavour, then the dish's creamy element); but if you're having butternut squash soup with ginger, chilli and coriander, you'd be better off with an Alsace Pinot Gris or an Australian Verdelho (again, first taking into account the intensity of flavour, then the dish's aromatic elements).

So... lots to consider. But if in doubt, just remember the golden rule: don't overpower one with the other. And some people will hate me for saying this, but if all else fails, there's a nugget of truth in that famous old adage: 'Red wine with red meat, white wine with white meat and fish.' Just don't live by it.

Some reliable pairings

Starters/Appetizers

ASPARAGUS	Condrieu, dry Muscat, Loire Sauvignon Blanc, fino Sherry
CHARCUTERIE/COLD CUTS	Beaujolais, Chinon, Bourgogne Pinot Noir, fino Sherry
CHICKEN LIVER PÂTE	Lightly oaked Chardonnay or amontillado Sherry
ROASTED MUSHROOMS	German, French or Oregon Pinot Noir, Langhe Nebbiolo
SNAILS IN GARLIC BUTTER	Aligoté, or a simple white Burgundy such as a Mâcon

Eggs

CHEESE OMELETTE WITH HERBS	Unoaked Chardonnay, Verdicchio
QUICHE LORRAINE	Pinot Blanc or Pinot Gris; or light reds like Saumur
COOKED BREAKFAST	Champagne (It cuts through the grease and wakes you up)

Easy suppers/snack meals

CHILLI CON CARNE	Big reds: Zinfandel, Cabernet Sauvignon, Ribera del Duero
HAMBURGERS	Medium–full juicy reds: Merlot, Grenache, Shiraz
PIZZA	Chianti, Merlot (better to match the topping)
SPAGHETTI BOLOGNESE	Chianti, Chilean Cabernet Sauvignon, South African red

Fish

CLAM CHOWDER	Oaked Chardonnay
CRAB	Riesling, Chablis, Muscadet sur lie
FISH & CHIPS	Australian Semillon Sauvignon; Champagne
FISH PIE WITH A CREAM SAUCE	Languedoc whites, Portuguese whites
LOBSTER	Alsace Riesling, white Rhône, white Burgundy
MUSSELS IN TOMATO SAUCE	California Sauvignon Blanc, Muscadet

Fish, continued

OYSTERS	Chablis, Muscadet, Champagne
SALADE NIÇOISE	Provence rosé
SMOKED SALMON	Alsace Riesling, Pouilly-Fuissé
SOLE	White Burgundy, Sancerre
TROUT	Chablis, white Bordeaux, Vouvray
TUNA	Cabernet Franc, Tavel Rosé

Meat & poultry

CARPACCIO OF BEEF	Rich whites; light to medium reds: Pinot Noir
GAME BIRDS	Red Burgundy, Nebbiolo, oloroso Sherry
RABBIT WITH HERBS	Red Burgundy; full-bodied white Châteauneuf
RIBS	Shiraz, Zinfandel, California Cabernets
ROAST BEEF	Big red: Bordeaux, Aussie Cabernet Sauvignon, Shiraz
ROAST CHICKEN	Usually white: Burgundy, Aussie Chardonnay
ROAST DUCK	Full-bodied Pinot Noir: Gevrey-Chambertin; Merlot: St-Emilion, Pomerol, Western Australia
ROAST LAMB	Medium- to full-bodied reds, e.g. Rioja
ROAST PORK	New World Pinot Noir, Barbera, Grenache-based reds
WILD BOAR	Châteauneuf, Languedoc and southern Italian reds

Cheeses

BLUE CHEESE	Sweet whites or reds, including Port
GOATS CHEESE	Sauvignon Blanc, Riesling, fruity rosés
HARD YELLOW CHEESE	Medium-bodied reds: St-Emilion, Grenache, amontillado Sherry
SOFT CHEESE	Beaujolais or Pinot Noir for Brie styles; off-dry aromatic whites for more powerful cheeses

Desserts

CHOCOLATE MOUSSE	Tawny Port, Banyuls, sweet Madeira
CHRISTMAS PUDDING	Port, sweet Madeira, sweet oloroso Sherry
FRUIT TART	Most fruity, sweet whites, especially Sauternes
CRÈME CARAMEL	Liqueur Muscat, tawny Port
CRÈME BRÛLÉE	Sweet Loire whites, sweet Muscats
FRESH ORCHARD FRUITS	Sweet Loire whites, off-dry or sweet Champagne
FRESH SUMMER BERRIES	Rosé Champagne, sweet Riesling
LEMON TART	Jurançon, Sauternes, sweet Riesling
SUMMER PUDDING	Sweet Muscat
TARTE TATIN	Coteaux de Layon, Sauternes
VANILLA ICE CREAM	Pedro Ximénez Sherry, Liqueur Muscat

Wine for the exotic East

When it comes to countries without a long-standing wine culture, it can be more difficult to match wines with their cuisine. It's hard not to generalize, but try the following.

CHINESE FOOD New World Sauvignon Blancs, Rueda, unoaked Chardonnays and Riesling in white; fruity Merlots, New World Pinot Noir, New World rosés can also be a good match. Or lager.

THAI FOOD Riesling and Gewürztraminer are good bets, as are Sauvignon Blancs. In red, young and fruity is a safe choice. Or lager.

INDIAN FOOD Fruity New World reds, but nothing too big and alcoholic; it all gets a bit overpowering otherwise, and the wine doesn't refresh you. Also, try flavourful New World whites, particularly Aussie and South African. Sparkling wines can be good, particularly ones with a hint of sweetness. Or lager.

JAPANESE FOOD Sake (a whole world to discover in itself); Sauvignon Blanc, Chablis, dry Sherry. Pinot Noir from Burgundy and New Zealand. Or lager.

IN THE
restaurant

According to a lot of people I've spoken to, this is the bit they don't like about wine. It's easy enough to select a bottle in a wine shop; you can just opt for a style you know and love, or if you do want to experiment, then you can read the labels and make an educated guess. Not so with the restaurant wine list: there is just a list of names in black and white. To make it even more taxing, we often feel the pressure of 'getting it right'. To top that off, all the wines on the list are much more expensive than in the shops. Triple whammy.

This is what leads people to what's referred to in the UK as the 'Englishman's Choice': the second bottle down the list, the one after the house wine. The Englishman's Choice has a threefold benefit:

1 It gives the impression you are making an informed choice, rather than just going for the house wine.

2 If you were to choose the house wine, it might make you look tight.

3 It's nice and cheap, which is a bonus, because you're secretly a bit tight.

No matter how safe this feels, it really isn't the best approach.

How to negotiate the wine list

The first thing to consider is: 'Are there lots of us?' If there are, everyone will be ordering different things, so try to get something that will go with the style of food in general as well as with a broad selection of dishes. If you're eating in an Italian restaurant, for instance, then you're probably best off going with something Italian, which will handle some stronger flavours but not stomp all over some more delicate ones. On the whole, you're probably better off choosing something medium-bodied, nothing too weird or unusual: a crowd-pleaser. If there's a big bunch of you, unless you're there specifically for the wine, there's not much point in going for the greatest bottles because...

1 you'll need lots of them to go around, and

2 you won't be able to give the wine that much attention anyway.

If there are just a couple or a few of you, though, then you might want to get something to match your food, or something special, unusual or interesting that will add to the enjoyment of the occasion. But, if you're each eating something completely different, you're unlikely to find a wine that will match everything effectively. The key here is for you all to order the same dish or something of a similar strength of flavour – or else choose the wine first, then the food to match it.

So you know the strength of flavour of the wine you want.
• Now think: 'Red or white?' Decide.
• Then think: 'Old World or New World?' Decide.

And that should have eliminated about 75% of the list, giving you a few suitable possibilities to choose from. Obviously, this is just one way of approaching it – far from the only or even the best way, but it can be useful.

A few words about prices

Restaurants make a lot of profit on drinks. When it comes to wine, they often work on a 2.5–3x mark-up on the retail price (expensive restaurants sometimes even more, particularly at the cheaper end of the list). So a wine that is £6 in the shops will probably cost around £15–£18. This is why you tend to see wines in restaurants you don't see in the shops, because otherwise you'd be able to compare the prices, which would lead to a feeling of mild outrage, and that isn't going to add much to the dining experience.

More restaurant-goers are aware of the price of food ingredients, so it's easier for restaurateurs to inflate the wine prices. Restaurant-owners argue that they make little money on food by the time it has been prepared and served, so they have to make higher margins on wine to pay for overheads. Admittedly, running a restaurant is an expensive business, and owners of independent restaurants are rarely millionaires. By artificially inflating just the price of wine, however, it's wine-lovers who end up subsidizing everyone else's dinner. All rather strange, considering it takes expertise to cook restaurant-quality food, but relatively little to uncork a bottle of wine. But the reality is that if you spend £15 on a bottle of wine in a restaurant, chances are it's worth about £5–£6, so expect this level of quality. You have to spend much more in a restaurant to get a reasonable bottle.

THE ENORMOUS
wine list

At certain restaurants, you'll be given a wine list so big you can hardly lift it. Here are a few pointers to help you cope.

• Chances are about two-thirds of it will be Bordeaux and Burgundy. If you don't want these, that cuts 66% of the list straight off. If it's a massive list, prices are likely to be equally massive in Burgundy and Bordeaux. Ask yourself: 'Is a rich person paying?' This will help you decide whether to leave in this big section.

• Don't read it all. Use the index, decide what styles you think could work, then refer to those sections. Don't wander into other areas or you'll be there all day.

• Choose a couple of styles that might work, then make a decision or ask the sommelier for his or her thoughts on your shortlist.

• Or just ask the sommelier for recommendations.

Sommeliers

The sommelier is the person in the restaurant you consult for wine suggestions, information and advice. In practice, the sommelier's job tends to involve looking after all aspects of the wine side of the operation: researching wines for the list, sourcing and purchasing, organizing storage both on and off the premises, looking after glassware, ensuring the wines are ready to drink, consulting with the kitchen to ensure the wines complement the food and so on. The sommelier should know at least some basic details about every wine on the wine list, and how each should work with any proposed dish. Only top restaurants can afford to take the wine side of things this seriously, though. Often, in smaller places, the restaurant manager will fulfil this role.

I remember being taken by my girlfriend to Le Manoir aux Quat'Saisons, Raymond Blanc's restaurant in Oxfordshire, for a surprise lunch for my 21st birthday. We were poor students, but she had saved for the occasion, and it was the best restaurant I had ever been to by a long, long way. I actually had to suppress a laugh when we were presented with the wine list, it was so big. Obviously I tried not to look like a complete muppet, opened it and started trying to read – and many of the wines appeared to be the same thing written over and over again, just with ascending prices. Almost all of them cost at least three figures, which was potentially ruinous. I must have looked very out of place: a young bloke with a shaved head sitting there in his dad's smart shoes leafing through this huge leather-bound tome. The sommelier came over, and within a few minutes, we told him what we were going to eat and he came out with a few different suggestions, all around the £25 mark (cheapest on the menu) without making us feel stingy or clueless. His choice was delicious: a red Mercurey from Burgundy that went brilliantly with the food.

A good sommelier should make you feel welcome and at ease, gauge what price band you want, guide you towards a selection of possibilities if necessary, or simply give you some background info on particular wines, or on the one you've chosen. Even if you've never heard of any of the styles, let alone individual bottles, a sommelier should make you feel like it was all your idea to try that particular bottle, which will definitely work with your dish, and how clever you are for spotting it.

For some reason, however, these wine waiters often have a bad name, but I've rarely had any bad experiences when dealing with them. They normally understand that most people eating in restaurants have limited knowledge when it comes to wine, and they should be trained to be helpful and tactful.

Sommeliers tend to be mines of knowledge about the wines on their list and come up with some good suggestions.

On occasion, however, they have tried to railroad me into buying wines above my stated budget. If they start this with you, just thank them for their suggestions and say you'd like some more time to look at the list yourself. You're under no obligation to go for anything they suggest, or even to listen to anything they say. Remember: you're the boss. You do sometimes hear stories about sommeliers or wine waiters kicking up a fuss when you send a wine back because it's faulty, but don't let this deter you if there is a genuine problem.

There are a couple of reasons you might want to send a wine back.

• It's not what you ordered. The waiter should present the bottle to you before she or he opens it. Check that it's the right one – not a £500 bottle of Bordeaux picked up by mistake. Because once you've said you want it and he opens it, it will be tricky to send it back once you've drunk it.

• It's faulty: either oxidized or corked. See Chapter 2 (page 28) for how to tell if you're unsure. The waiter should offer to let you taste it before it's poured around the table so that you can check. It's nobody's fault if it is corked; you simply get a bad one sometimes, what with it being a natural product kept in a bottle sealed with a bit of old tree. If there is something wrong with it, say so politely and ask for a replacement. There should be no argument; if there is, just explain which of the above faults is apparent, and that should clear things up.

6

HOT CHAMPAGNE
OUT of A MUG

HOW TO GET
THE most
OUT OF YOUR
BOTTLE

I t might make sense to assume that when it comes to wine, the most essential thing is choosing the right bottle, but that only gets it as far as your kitchen. Wine is a fragile, natural substance; just because it has a reputation for lasting for years doesn't mean that it's in any way robust. Wine does need to be treated with care if you want to keep it happy.

Getting it into your mouth in the right state is equally important. The things that make the biggest difference here are its serving temperature and what you drink it out of. I'd prefer a chilled glass of Aussie sparkling wine any day to a splash of warm Champagne from a disposable plastic cup. If you can't smell it or taste it properly, then what's the point? Opening the bottle without getting bits of cork in the wine, and pouring it so that you avoid any sediment also help. Altogether, these things make a huge difference to the amount of enjoyment you get out of each bottle.

WINE
storage

Most of us just buy a bottle of wine as and when we need one. Most of the rest of us buy a few at a time, or maybe a dozen, and store them in a rack at home, pulling them out when required. Only a tiny fortunate few have any kind of purpose-built cellar or temperature-regulated storage cabinet.

If you're keeping wine for more than a month or two, though, it pays to store the bottles the right way; otherwise there's a chance that they might not be quite as you remember them when it comes time to pull the cork.

 FIRST, store them on their side. This keeps any corks wet and swollen, reducing the chance of air getting in and oxidizing your wine.

 SECOND, keep the bottles somewhere cool. Between 10–13°C is perfect, but anywhere pretty cool should be fine (the warmer it is, the faster the wine will develop in the bottle). It's more important that there are no big temperature fluctuations, so the shed, the loft or next to the cooker are all bad ideas.

3 **THIRD,** keep them away from direct natural or artificial light.

4 **FINALLY,** keep bottles away from vibration – so away from the boiler, the dishwasher and the washing machine.

If you're buying cases of wine that need long-term aging, such as red Bordeaux or vintage Port, you might be better off putting them in a professional wine-storage warehouse. The owners will charge a small amount per case per year to look after things, but they keep your bottles in perfect condition. For short-term storage, the bottom of the wardrobe works well enough for me.

WINE corkscrews

When it comes to opening wine bottles, there have been dozens of different corkscrew designs over the centuries, but naturally only the fittest have survived. There are only a few styles left these days in the shops. The most common is the wing corkscrew. This is the one with two levers on either side that rise as you screw in the 'worm' (the twisty bit), then you pull them down and that pulls out the cork. These are next in line to becoming extinct. You can't get any accuracy with the worm, which is always too thick, and the whole thing makes stupid clanking noises like a bored ghost.

The other one you see a lot is the waiter's friend (the one that resembles a penknife). This is the most practical, because of its foldaway mechanism, and the handy little knife that you use to cut off the foil. You can be quite accurate with this one, although it does take a bit of practice.

One good one is the big 'rabbit'-style contraption (stop giggling at the back) that looks like a torture device – the one with the two arms you clamp around the bottle neck, that has the lever you pull down towards you, then up again to remove the cork. It's quick and easy, but – most importantly – the worm is thin, goes directly down the centre of the cork and pulls it directly upwards, which is useful for extracting crumbly corks from older bottles (so it's particularly suited to Port-lovers).

Ever settled down with a girl/guy, found somewhere quiet to chill for the evening, brought along a bottle of wine, even remembered to bring some glasses – then discovered you forgot the corkscrew? Take heart. Frustrating as it is, this need not result in getting no action.

1 The 'poke-it-in' method

Get a stick/lighter/pen as thick as your little finger. Put base of wine bottle on the ground between your feet. Hold neck of bottle. Push cork into neck of bottle. Use poking device to stop cork bobbing up into the neck and getting in the way when pouring the wine.

DOWNSIDE The wine is likely to gush up like a fountain out of the bottle all over you unless done with consummate skill. Fortunately, by the end of the bottle, it seems to matter less that you're a bit damp.

2 The 'bang-it-on-the-wall' method

Get a newspaper, fold it in half to make a thick pad. Hold pad against a wall. Bang base of wine bottle against pad very hard over and over and over again. Eventually the cork will start popping up. Grip with teeth and pull out.

DOWNSIDE Your neighbours will hate you and your teeth will hurt.

3 The sabre method

Select a heavy sabre. Find the seam/join on the neck of your bottle of Champagne. Hold the base of the bottle. Run the back of your sabre up the bottle firmly until it hits the lip of the neck of the bottle. The force should break the top off the bottle around the cork, with the wine washing away any shards of glass.

DOWNSIDE You need a heavy sabre. You risk cutting off your thumb. You risk striking those around you with a sabre. You risk hitting someone with the end that flies off. You risk weakening the bottle, which could shatter. Apart from that, perfectly safe.

There is one other method, which is the 'smash the top off, then drink from the jagged glass method'. A friend of mine tried this. He wouldn't advise it.

WINE
glasses

The shape of the glass makes *a lot* of difference to the amount of enjoyment you get from your wine. The most important thing is that the glass is shaped more like a U than a V. If it's a U-shape – or, even better, a tulip shape that tapers back in at the top – then when you swirl the wine around the glass, the aromas will stay enclosed. This way, you can stick your nose in and hoover them up to see what they smell like. If it's a V-shape, you won't be able to swirl the wine around to release the aromas without it going everywhere, and as soon as any aromas have been released, there's nothing to stop them dissipating into the atmosphere before you get your nose in.

And yes, a glass *does* have to be glass. Plastic smells slightly of plastic and whatever else has ever been in it beforehand, while metal can react unfavourably with wine. Glass is not only inert, but it's usually clear, meaning you can see whether there is any deposit, cloudiness, fizziness, etc., and you can get a good look at the colour. You don't have to shell out a fortune on tasting glasses; any tulip-shaped one with a stem will do. You need the stem so that you can hold the glass without warming up the wine with your fingers. And this goes for all wines. You may have seen little thimble-sized glasses for tasting Sherry and Port. If you encounter these, please smash them immediately. When it comes to tasting wines – *all* wines – your nose is what gives you the most pleasure.

You need to be able to swirl your wine around, release its aromas and get your nose in there to smell them.

You just can't do this with those pathetic little schooner things. Whether it's Port, Sherry, Madeira, claret, Sauternes or whatever, use decent-sized wine glasses. Champagne flutes are also good at delivering the aromas to your nose, but you still need some space to give it a swirl, so don't overfill them.

What's the right glass at a restaurant?

At restaurants, there can be a range of different glassware on the table. The biggest glass is for red wines, which sometimes need some extra coaxing to release their aromas, particularly when young. The smaller, tulip-shaped glass is most often for the white wine. Water glasses tend not to have a stem.

WINE
temperature

Temperature makes a huge difference to a wine's flavour: just taste the same bottle at different temperatures. The right temperature means getting wine bottles nice and cool. Not just whites and rosés, but reds as well. Of course, whites and rosés are always better cold. Straight from the refrigerator and you won't get much in terms of aroma, but as they warm up they'll start playing ball.

It's also worth chilling reds a little before opening them: just 20 minutes or so makes all the difference. The average room temperature of 20–25°C is too warm for most red wines; it makes alcohol more prominent, flavours less defined and the drink less refreshing, so 16–18°C is better. Some reds can be chilled even more, particularly the lightest: it accentuates their freshness and acidity. Serve sparkling wines and sweet white wine cold, sweet reds like Port and Banyuls slightly chilled, and tawny Ports and sweet Madeiras chilled or at room temperature.

WINE
decanters

There are two reasons to decant a wine. The first is to aerate it, which 'opens it up'. This is done to younger wines, which sometimes need a bit of coaxing before they'll release their aromas. It's normally just done with reds, but powerful whites also benefit. Simply pour the wine into a decanter and leave it uncovered for as long as possible – preferably two or three hours. By 'decanter' I don't necessarily mean a cut-glass ornament; a clean water jug is just as good.

The second reason to decant a wine is to remove any sediment that might have built up over time. This occurs in big red wines with some age, when the compounds in the wine clump together over time and fall out of suspension. It's harmless, but gritty. In this case, stand the bottle up for as long as possible so that the sediment falls to the bottom. Then pour slowly into the decanting vessel until you get to the end and start to see a bit of sludge coming out – then stop. A tea strainer can be handy here to catch any bits. If it's a very old wine, rinse out the bottle with cold water and pour the wine back in – they don't like too much contact with air.

7

TIME to EXPLORE

N ext time you're choosing a wine, don't go for the usual. Try something you've never had before. Consider the German ones. Seek out the sweet ones. Sniff out the old ones. Chances are they wouldn't sell it if it were *that* weird. The biggest problem these days is finding one that's weird enough!

Better still, try a different shop, or drop into a supermarket and see what it has. Best of all, have a quick geek around on the internet, find your nearest independent wine shop and order a selection by post. If you need guidance, just ask – they should be happy to help. Below are a few suggestions to point you in the right direction if you feel like trying something new, as well as some tips on how to find some gems via tastings, wine clubs and wineries.

IF YOU LIKE THIS,
you might like that

Reds

If you like Cabernet Sauvignon, try Shiraz, Malbec, Zinfandel

If you like Syrah, try Tempranillo, Touriga Nacional, Barbera

If you like Merlot, try Grenache/Garnacha, Dolcetto, Mourvèdre

If you like Sangiovese (Chianti), try Cabernet Franc, Mencía, Cinsault

If you like Pinot Noir, try Nebbiolo, Gamay, Dornfelder

Whites

If you like Chardonnay, try Pinot Blanc, Chenin Blanc, Marsanne

If you like Sauvignon Blanc, try Sémillon, Riesling, Grüner Veltliner

If you like Pinot Grigio, try Fiano, Gavi, unoaked Chardonnay

If you like Viognier, try Gewürztraminer, Sylvaner, dry Muscat

SOME WINES
grouped by style

If you like one in each group, you might like the others.

LIGHT, FRESH, CRISP WHITES
- Sancerre
- Chablis
- Muscadet
- Vinho Verde
- Gavi
- White Rioja *joven*

MEDIUM-BODIED WHITES
- Albariño
- Alsace or Oregon Pinot Gris
- Austrian Grüner Veltliner
- Most Viognier
- South African or
  Loire Chenin Blanc

BIG, RICH WHITES
- Portuguese whites
- White Rioja *reserva/gran reserva*
- White Bordeaux
- Powerful white Burgundies such as
  Meursault, Chassagne-Montrachet
- Powerful white Rhône such as
  Hermitage Blanc, Condrieu

FLORAL AND/OR AROMATIC WHITES
- Gewürztraminer
- Sylvaner
- Riesling
- Dry Muscat
- Lebanese whites

WHITES WITH A HINT OF SWEETNESS
- Some Vouvrays
- Most German Rieslings
  (unless it says *trocken* ['dry']
  on the label)

SWEET WHITES
- Sauternes
- Barsac
- German Auslese/Beerenauslese/
  Trockenbeerenauslese
- Eiswein/Icewine
- Tokáji
- Sweet Loire whites such as
  Bonnezeaux, Coteaux du Layon
  or Quarts-de-Chaume
- Muscat de Beaumes-de-Venise

Whites

LIGHT, FRESH REDS
- Bourgogne Pinot Noir
- Pinot Noir from the Loire, Germany, Alsace, Oregon
- Beaujolais-Villages
- Valpolicella
- Bardolino

MEDIUM-WEIGHT REDS
- Red Burgundy from named villages
- Pinot Noir from California, Chile, South Africa, Australia
- Inexpensive Bordeaux
- Red Côtes-du-Rhône
- Chianti
- Rioja *crianza*
- Chinon
- Bourgueil

BIG, POWERFUL REDS
- *Grand cru* red Burgundy
- Young *cru classé* Bordeaux
- Cornas and Hermitage
- Rioja *reserva/gran reserva*
- Portuguese reds
- Aglianico
- Zinfandel
- Carmenère
- California Cabernet Sauvignon
- Argentinian Malbec
- Barolo and Barbaresco

(NB red wines become less big and powerful as they age, so if any of the above are at least 12 years old, they can be put in the 'medium-weight' category)

SWEET REDS
- Banyuls
- Red Port

Reds

LIGHT, SUBTLE ROSÉS
- Provence rosé
- Corsican rosé

ROSÉS WITH A HINT OF SWEETNESS
- Anjou rosé
- Some English rosé

ROSÉS WITH SOME POWER
- Most New World rosé
- Italian Cerasuolo
- Spanish rosé

Rosés

OTHER WAYS
to explore

Home or restaurants aren't the only options when it comes to enjoying wine. There are lots of other ways you can get your lips around some tasty morsels.

Tastings

Wine tastings come in a number of different forms. At their most basic, they're just ad-hoc small plastic taster glasses of a wine being handed out in a shop or supermarket. Or they may be more organized, perhaps with a selection of wines to try from a producer where you can take a bit more time, maybe with someone who can tell you something about what you're drinking.

Wine tastings might be arranged by your workplace or college as a social event or reward.

They can be organized informally in-house: just a hired room with a table with a bunch of wines to taste, or with specialists brought in to host the event. The more structured, formal wine tastings can be tutored or untutored. If untutored, the tasting is likely to consist of a few groups (or 'flights') of wines, possibly grouped by region or grape variety, with some notepaper for you to write down which ones you like and which you don't. If it is tutored, there will be someone to talk you through them and give you some information about how they are made.

Larger wine tastings, like annual range tasting put on by independent wine shops, or ones organized by wine magazines, tend to be in massive venues with dozens of tables dotted around the room with a producer standing behind each one offering his or her range of wines for you to taste. Just go up to the person behind the stand and tell them which ones you'd like to try. The bigger events feel more like corporate exhibitions, with professionally produced stands, smiling staff and big logo banners. They can be a good laugh, but start early, because they can get rowdy by the end. Or go at the end and prepare to get rowdy.

Wine clubs

Wine clubs are a great way of keeping informed about what's going on: new wines being released, new vintages, tastings, etc. A number of supermarkets and wine-shop chains have their own wine clubs, which can be handy for hearing about discounts and the like. Independent wine-shop wine clubs will have more of a DIY feel about them, but on the whole you'll come across much more interesting wines and tastings with them. They frequently host visiting winemakers, who can be fascinating people to meet, and from whom you can really find out about all the nitty-gritty behind the label. They tend to love showing off their top wines, too: the ones you can rarely afford to buy or find an excuse to open.

There are also other local wine clubs run either by small groups of wine enthusiasts just for the love of it, or by small local businesses. If you work for a medium to large company, it may also have a wine club. In the UK, for example, some of the big banks and energy companies have well-attended ones that get through some subsidized quality stuff. Not to be sniffed at.

Visiting wineries

The best way to get a feel for the whole process is to visit a winery, and this is easily arranged. There are wineries in all wine-producing areas that have full tour-and-tasting facilities and accept visitors all year round, even in the UK. Have a quick look on the internet to see if any are near you or easy to get to (and see Appendix 1, page 184, in this book for more information). Give them a quick call in advance to check if they're open or whether you need to book, and see if any events are coming up that are worth catching.

Visiting wineries abroad can be even more fascinating, since some of them are ancient and have been in families for centuries. Visiting a vast commercial winery in Napa, a Sherry *bodega* in Jerez, a *grande marque* Champagne house, or a small grower in Burgundy will each deliver a different experience and a new perspective.

WINERY

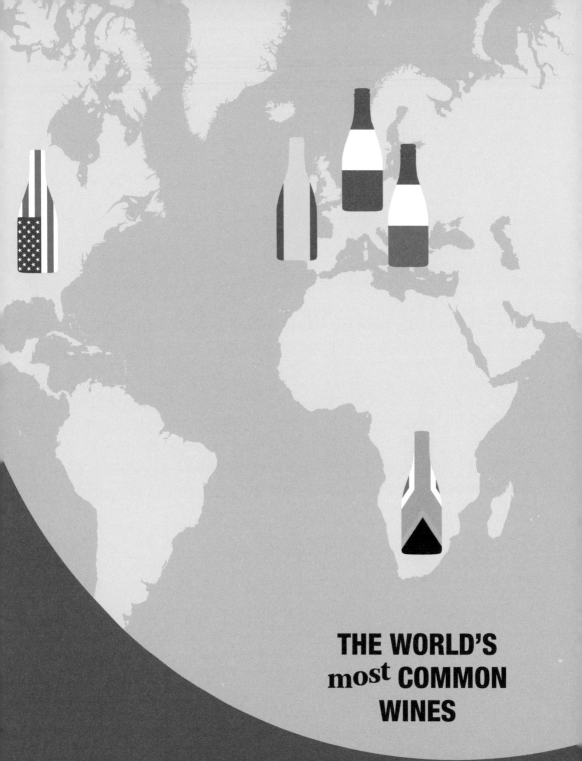

THE WORLD'S most COMMON WINES

PART 2

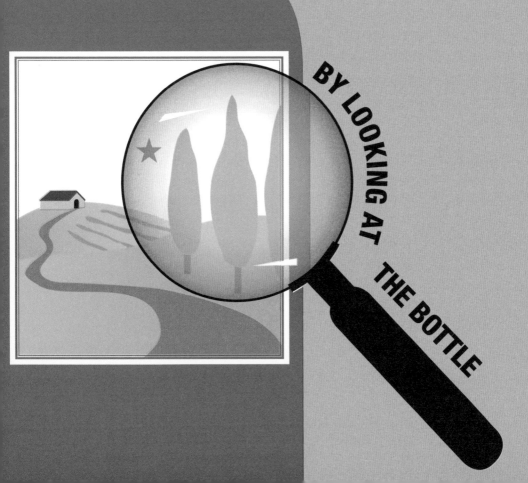

8

HOW TO TELL WHAT IT will TASTE LIKE

BY LOOKING AT THE BOTTLE

n the first part of this book, we looked at what wine is and how it's made, how best to taste and enjoy it with friends, where to get the best bottles and how to get the most out of it in terms of serving and matching it with food. But when you walk into a supermarket or a wine shop, how do you know the difference between one wine and the next? It's hard not to be swayed by how much you like a label, yet the designer who creates the label might not even have tasted the wine, so labels are far from reliable indicators. The second part of the book tells you about the most common types of wine you'll encounter in shops and restaurants, and what to expect from typical examples. Hopefully this will provide a useful starting point for figuring out what might float your boat and which areas you might enjoy exploring.

When trying to decide what any particular bottle might taste like, the most important things to remember are:

1 **THE REGION, AND**   *2* **THE GRAPE VARIETY**

After these two, knowing a bit about vintages and, most of all, individual producers, will help you find the best examples. Within each region, it's the combination of natural elements that creates the difference between one wine and the next.

• **CLIMATE** The amount of sunlight, temperature and rainfall. This can differ from region, to vineyard, to individual plants.

• **TOPOGRAPHY** Altitude (the higher you go, the colder it gets), relief (i.e. what direction the vineyard faces) and angle of slope.

• **GEOLOGY** The type of soil or soils (topsoil, subsoil, etc.).

These elements combine to create what the French call *terroir* (pronounced *tare-wah*). In theory, these quasi-static, unmalleable, natural elements give a sense of place to a wine, despite different vintages or winemaking practices. There's a lot of debate about exactly what terroir is – and even whether or not it exists at all.

In his book *The Art and Science of Wine,* venerated wine-writer Hugh Johnson paraphrases winemaker Peter Sichel by saying that a wine's character is derived from its terroir, its quality from its winemaker, and its personality from the vintage. This is a useful way of looking at things.

GRAPE
varieties

Every grape variety has its own particular character and flavour profile, and some are happier in certain parts of the world than others. Certain varieties rarely grow successfully outside one small region. An example of this is the Nebbiolo grape, which is widely planted in Piemonte (Piedmont, in northeastern Italy), where it is used to make Barolo and Barbaresco, two of the most extraordinary wines you'll ever come across. But it pretty much refuses to make half-decent wine anywhere else.

Some varieties grow happily in many different regions but always let the particular terroir shine through.

Chardonnay is a classic example of this, because it is grown all over the world but often with easily identifiable regional characteristics. Other grapes, such as Cabernet Sauvignon, have very strong characters and are always immediately identifiable, no matter where they're grown.

Most of the more common varieties you'll come across are indigenous to Old World countries, so they remain strongly connected with particular regions: Cabernet Sauvignon with Bordeaux, for example, or Sangiovese with Chianti, Pinot Noir with Burgundy, and so on. You'll find each grape variety's typical flavour profile and character within the relevant regional chapters in this book.

At the start of each country chapter is a list of grape varieties. These are the varieties used to make most of the wines that get exported, rather than the most widely planted. So if you know you like Cabernet Sauvignon or Riesling, for example, you'll know straight away that these chapters are definitely worth a look.

WINE STYLES
still, sparkling, fortified, sweet

The vast majority of wines you'll encounter are dry still reds, whites and rosés, and these are covered within their country of origin. First, however, by way of an 'apéritif' (i.e. before-dinner drink), we'll have a look at Champagne and sparkling wines, which I've grouped together to explain how and where they're made. Similarly, fortified and sweet wines are grouped together at the end of the main section as a kind of after-dinner treat to round everything off.

Like sparkling wines, fortified and sweet styles also involve very different processes of production that have a big impact on the taste of the finished wine. Additionally, they tend to have different 'uses': fortified and sweet wines are usually drunk after a meal, or paired with specific types of food, such as nibbles, desserts, and certain hard-to-match dishes.

Sweet and fortified wines are almost always grouped together where they are sold. Because they are often packaged quite differently to both still and sparkling wines, it's unlikely that you would buy one of these unwittingly while looking for a bottle of dry still white or red – or indeed a bottle of bubbly to get the party started.

Whatever style of wine you're considering, however, within each is a huge variety of different flavours that you just won't find anywhere else.

OLD WORLD
vs new world

'Old World' means mostly European countries that have made wines for centuries: France, Germany, Spain, Portugal, Italy, Greece, etc. 'New World' refers to those such as the US, Chile, Argentina, Australia, New Zealand and South Africa that have exported quality bottled wine for just a few decades. In general, Old World wines are light to full-bodied, subtle and refined, with savoury fruit flavours and light to medium alcohol. New World wines tend to be medium- to full-bodied (sometimes *very* full-bodied) with bright, concentrated, ripe, fruit flavours and medium to high alcohol.

Of course, it's far from this clear cut. Some big, fruity southern French wines might be mistaken for Australian. And wines from the coolest New World countries can rarely be described as concentrated, ripe and fruity. Nonetheless, 'Old World/New World' is a useful place to start when choosing a wine.

But just because the Old World has made wine longer doesn't mean the New World can't produce quality wines. When you're looking for something special, don't default to France, Spain or Italy; there's a lot of top-notch Californian, Australian, and South African wine out there. Even so, the New World chapters in this book aren't as long as those dedicated to the Old World, and there are a couple of other reasons for this:

1 Compared to the Old World, there tend to be fewer widely recognized New World subregions with distinct winemaking traditions, as well as a lot less regulation, particularly in countries newer to wine production.

2 Many New World countries stick to a smaller number of better-known grapes and often make varietal (single grape-variety) wines that focus on the grape rather than the growing region.

Old World traditions: pros and cons

France, Italy and other Old World countries have produced wine for thousands of years. They've had huge numbers of indigenous varieties to choose from, and these have grown and adapted to suit particular environments. Also, wines have been made for many different purposes, sometimes pushed in stylistic directions to work with regional foods. Such wines have often developed in relative independence, using specific techniques and methods – which is why many Old World wines are remnants of older ways of life, highly specific in style, sometimes created to match specialized regional cuisines. This is the joy of the Old World: wines at the extremities of production are frequently more 'bizarre' than their New World counterparts, often using pretty odd methods that wouldn't make sense today.

However, this has disadvantages. For the person in the supermarket trying to decide what will go with dinner, Old World wines are harder to understand. This is because originally wine wasn't consumed in numerous countries; it was made and drunk locally. There was no back label explaining how it tasted; locals knew how local wine tasted because it was all they drank. Among some smaller producers, this parochial attitude still prevails: 'Why should I put "Chardonnay" on my Chablis label? *All* Chablis is made from Chardonnay, and everyone knows what it tastes like: it's the finest white in the world." OK, so Chablis is a great wine, and the locals know what it's like. But how is John in Manchester supposed to know when he's in the local wine shop wondering what to take to his girlfriend's place?

New World innovation: closing the gap

When it came to making wine, the New World had an immediate advantage. In most cases these countries didn't have centuries of baggage. They didn't have to stick to local weirdo varieties, or have bad habits ingrained into their production methods. They weren't restricted by tradition, local rules and regulations. They simply looked at other successful winemaking areas and replicated what they saw. Obviously, it wasn't as easy as that; selecting good sites for the right grapes was necessary, as was learning to combat new diseases, pests and climatic challenges. But being open to innovation and experimentation led to a whole new world of wine.

Because these new wines weren't part of a culinary tradition, as in France or Spain, they needed to explain what was *in* a bottle in order to sell it. Stating the grape variety on the label was the best way of letting buyers know what a wine tasted like, and the producer's name gave an indication of quality. To begin with, there wasn't that much else to say. People didn't know how a McLaren Vale Shiraz compared to a Barossa Shiraz (both in Australia), but what did mean something to consumers was that they liked Cabernet Sauvignon or Sauvignon Blanc, because each has a flavour profile that's more or less similar wherever it's made. And that Dr. Penfold made some pretty good stuff; as did Edward Tyrrell and Thomas Hardy. These names became brands, and branding began to play an increasingly important part in New World wine production. Suddenly, wine became easier to understand. Thanks to varietal labelling, people realized it was largely the grape that made a wine taste a certain way. And easy-to-remember brand names gave consumers confidence to buy wine of a reliable quality – not just another Château Something that looked just like Château Thingy but tasted completely different. So, with New World innovation, new technology, large-scale production methods and attractive labelling and branding, wine lost some of its obscure, esoteric aura. And people started drinking more of it.

Well, more New World wine, anyway. When Australia overtook France as the biggest exporter of wine to the UK, it was a wake-up call to the Old World's wine industry: it needed to haul itself into the twenty-first century if traditional winemaking countries were still going to compete. After some lessons in marketing from New World winemakers, today they're fighting back, with varietal labelling, more helpful back labels and improved packaging. As more winemakers reach out to the mass market, though, let's hope the fascinating, unusual and more idiosyncratic wines don't get pushed out altogether.

Winemaking traditions and regional specialities in the New World are developing as specific terroirs are recognized and there's increasing experimentation with less common grape varieties. The gap between Old and New World is starting to close. Some might argue that this 'world' way of categorizing wines is no longer even valid. But it remains helpful at present, even if we talk about 'New World style' and 'Old World style' rather than referring to specific countries.

THINGS TO CHECK ON A WINE LABEL
to find out what it contains

Alcohol levels

If you see a bottle of Old World still dry wine and its alcohol level is much more than 14% ABV, you might want to think twice if you don't know the producer, particularly if it's a white: the alcohol could be out of balance and it might taste 'hot'. Allow New World bottles a little extra leeway.

Where it's bottled

If a wine was bottled on the estate where it was made, this is a good thing, as it wasn't trucked in the sun to the bottling plant, which is unlikely to do it any favours. English labels will say something like 'estate bottled'; in French, it's *Mise en bouteille au château/domaine*. The terms 'reserve', *grand vin*, etc., can be used by anyone, though, so they don't mean anything important.

14% ABV

Grading system

Finally, most countries have a more or less official grading system of quality to help you know what to expect when you buy a bottle. To bring all European countries into line when it comes to labels' stated quality levels, the EU has created new bands for wines with an accepted regional or subregional style. Established wine regions can change their terminology to the new style if they want (and some already have), but it's not compulsory. Any newly designated wine regions will have to use the new terms, however, so both are listed below, to cover whatever you'll encounter on a wine label.

	1	2	3	4	5
FRANCE NEW	Vin	Indication Géographique Protégée (IGP)		Appellation d'Origine Protégée (AOP)	
FRANCE OLD	Vin de Table	Vin de Pays	Vin Délimité de Qualité Supérieur (VDQS)	Appellation (d'Origine) Contrôlée (AOC/AC)	
SPAIN NEW	Vino	Indicación Geográfica Protegida (IGP)		Denominación de Origen Protegida (DOP)	
SPAIN OLD	Vino de Mesa	Vino de la Tierra		Denominación de Origen (DO)	Denominación de Origen Calificada (DOCa)
ITALY NEW	Vino	Indicazione Geografica Protetta (IGP)		Denominazione di Origine Protetta (DOP)	
ITALY OLD	Vino da Tavola	Indicazione Geografica Tipica (IGT)		Denominazione di Origine Controllata (DOC)	Denominazione di Origine Controllata e Garantita (DOCG)
PORTUGAL NEW	Vinho	Indicação Geográfica Protegida (IGP)		Denominação de Origem Protegida (DOP)	
PORTUGAL OLD	Vinho de Mesa	Vinho Regional	Indicação de Proveniencia Regulamentada (IPR)	Denominação de Origem Controlada (DOC)	

Taking the (old) French system as the yardstick, you have the most basic of wines, the 'table wines' which, on the whole, are simple wines for quaffing. The second level up, in this case French *vin de pays*, or 'country wines', can be a source of decent-quality, inexpensive wines, and some fairly uninspiring bottles, too. Next up is somewhere between *vin de pays* and *appellation contrôlée*. The final, and generally highest quality level is the *appellation d'origine contrôlée* (AOC), or just *appellation contrôlée*. This is the most exacting in quality terms, and the best wines, or at least the well-known classic wines from each region, will be in this level. Spain is a little different in that it has no level 3 category; instead it has a higher level 5, but in practice, there's little difference in quality between its levels 4 and 5. Similarly, Italy skips level 2, and also has a level 5, but keeps this just for its most classic wines. This isn't to say that Italy and Spain make better wines than the others; they just grade them a little differently.

Each level is more and more rigorous as to exactly what you can do with your wine, dictating things such as the area in which you can grow grapes, what varieties are allowed, maximum yields, alcoholic strength, and some vineyard and winery practices. So if a winemaker just wants to make a simple, cheap wine – buying land outside any well-known region, planting an easy-to-grow but undistinguished grape variety (there are no restrictions at this level) – chances are that, by law, he could label it only *vin de table/vino de mesa/vino da tavola/vinho de mesa*. In order to put 'Chinon', 'Fleurie' or another appellation on his label, he'd have to stick to the legally recognized area – and to other stipulated rules particular to that area.

But just because a wine is AOC/DOC, etc., doesn't necessarily mean it will be excellent; it just means it should at least be recognizable as a Bordeaux or a Barolo or whatever it claims to be, and that the producer has met certain production standards.

If the winemaker is rubbish, the wine could still be crap, and just because a wine is a vin de pays *doesn't necessarily mean it will be average or poor quality.*

If a maverick genius from Chianti wants to add some Malbec into his wines, he won't be able to call the result a DOC Chianti because it won't tick all the legal boxes. This doesn't mean the wine will be poor quality; it could be delicious, but by law it has to be classed as a *vino da tavola*. That's the downside with these fairly rigid categories: although they should deliver a style of wine you expect from an appellation, there's little room for experimentation. At the end of the day, it's the producer that counts.

Germany, by the way, is a law unto itself, and grades its wines largely according to the sweetness of the juice that goes into it; *see* the Germany section (pages 132-3) for a full explanation. Other countries, such as those in North America, have grading systems, but they are often voluntary, very loose or still being developed, and so are less important to know about when choosing your wine.

A quick guide to countries and regions and what they do well

FRANCE
Potentially everything

ALSACE	Wonderful and varied aromatic whites, subtle reds
BEAUJOLAIS	Light to medium-bodied fruity reds
BORDEAUX	Potentially excellent reds, whites and sweet wines
BURGUNDY	Potentially excellent food-friendly medium-bodied reds and rich whites
CHABLIS	Very dry, crisp whites
CHAMPAGNE	The best sparkling wines in the world
LANGUEDOC-ROUSSILLON	Powerful, rustic reds and some good-value whites
LOIRE	Appetizing light to medium reds, good broad range of whites (some sweetish), good 'stickies' (i.e. sweet wines) and decent sparkling wine
PROVENCE	Excellent subtle rosés and full-bodied reds
NORTHERN RHÔNE	Medium-bodied to powerful, spicy reds and whites — some excellent
SOUTHERN RHÔNE	Soft, broad, approachable reds, some quite gutsy
SANCERRE	Expressive dry, aromatic whites

SPAIN
Some excellent medium to full reds, some decent fresh whites and agreeable fizz

GALICIA	Fruity, zesty whites
JEREZ (SHERRY)	Complex, food-friendly white wines often with a distinctive yeasty and/or oxidative flavour
RIBERA DEL DUERO	Full-bodied, powerful and polished reds
RIOJA	Medium to full reds, some excellent, varied styles. Oaky whites; not much fruit but potentially very interesting

GERMANY
Pure, zesty, potentially excellent whites, some delicate, complex reds

MOSEL	Laser-like, pure, high-acidity whites, often with a degree of sweetness
PFALZ	Various interesting aromatic whites and some enjoyable reds
RHEINGAU	Richer, pure, high-acidity whites

ITALY
Dry reds and whites, some decent sparklers

GAVI	Light, stylish, potentially good whites
MONTEPULCIANO & MONTALCINO	Medium- to full-bodied dry, sometimes herbal reds, potentially excellent
PIEMONTE/PIEDMONT	Medium-bodied to powerful complex tannic reds, Barolo and Barbaresco potentially amazing
TOSCANA/TUSCANY	Medium-weight, potentially excellent reds
SOUTHERN ITALY	Many rustic wines, some charming and characterful whites, some powerful and impressive reds
VENETO	Light to medium-bodied crisp reds, potentially very good. Soft, clean whites and some pleasant sparklers

PORTUGAL
Powerful reds; big whites.
Excellent sweet reds (Port)

SWITZERLAND
Expensive, subtle whites and reds

MADEIRA
Sweet and dry fortifieds

GREECE
Some good medium-bodied reds
and lovely herbal whites

AUSTRIA
Potentially brilliant dry whites,
potentially sumptuous reds

UK
Some decent whites, some very
good sparkling wines

HUNGARY
Chunky reds, dry whites and
fabulous sweet whites

LEBANON
Big, bold reds and
aromatic whites

NEW ZEALAND
Fresh, fruity aromatic whites; medium- to full-bodied reds

CENTRAL OTAGO	Some gorgeous Pinot Noir
HAWKE'S BAY	NZ's best non-Pinot Noir reds, medium- to full-bodied
MARLBOROUGH	Some very good whites and reds, and intense Sauvignon Blancs

AUSTRALIA
Potentially excellent medium- to full-bodied whites and reds, decent sparkling and some notable sweet wines

BAROSSA	Powerful reds
COONAWARRA	Very good medium to full-bodied reds
EDEN & CLARE VALLEYS	Excellent Riesling
HUNTER VALLEY	Characterful reds and whites
MCLAREN VALE	Big, silky reds, fruity whites
TASMANIA	Fresh whites, decent Pinot Noir and sparklers
WESTERN AUSTRALIA	Potentially excellent, less full-bodied in style
YARRA VALLEY	Good Pinot Noir

SOUTH AFRICA
Potentially good across the board, from medium to full reds to whites and sweet wines

CONSTANTIA	More elegant whites and reds, sweet wine
STELLENBOSCH	Good-quality region for reds

USA
Bold whites and reds, mostly single varieties

CALIFORNIA	Stunning varietal Napa Valley reds and whites; very good from Sonoma, too
OREGON	Some subtle, delicious Pinot Noirs
NEW YORK	Good Rieslings; subtle Chardonnay, Cabernet Sauvignon, Cabernet Franc
VIRGINIA	Full, fruity, polished reds and whites
WASHINGTON STATE	Intense reds, especially Merlot and good fuller-style Rieslings

CANADA
Good Pinot Noir, Riesling and icewine

CHILE
Good varietal wines; lots of value here

ARGENTINA
Great Malbec, Cabernet Sauvignon and Torrontés

OTHER LATIN AMERICA
Good-value varietals from Mexico, Uruguay and Brazil

9

**FIRST, AN
APERITIF:**

CHAMPAGNE and
SPARKLING WINES

B efore diving into the country-by-country sections of this book, let's examine a drink that knows no boundaries: fizz. Think 'celebration drink' and most people think 'Champagne'. Yet there are lots of sparkling wines: from French *crémants* and German *Sekt* to Spanish Cava and Italian Prosecco – not to mention New World sparklers. All have carbon dioxide dissolved in them. Remove the 'mushroom' cork and this gas bubbles out of the wine, making it fizz.

Bubbles get into wine in several ways; some methods affect taste as well as fizz. The fermentation that makes alcohol also makes carbon dioxide, or CO_2 (sugar + yeast = alcohol + CO_2). Normally, CO_2 just escapes into the air, but if fermentation occurs in a sealed container, the gas has nowhere to go, so it dissolves into the wine. This is how most decent sparkling wine is made. Some good sparklers are made via the 'tank method'; wine is put in a tank with yeast and sugar to cause a second fermentation, then bottled under pressure after the lees are removed (see page 16). A lot of New World fizz and most Italian Proseccos are made this way, and can result in enjoyable wines.

The best way to make sparkling wine, though, is with the méthode traditionnelle or méthode champenoise.

These terms mean the same thing, but the second can be used legally only within the Champagne region. In both cases, the second fermentation takes place in the wine bottle. It's attributed to Dom Pérignon, a 17th-century winemaking Bénédictine monk. He didn't 'invent' it as such; his main concern was actually removing the bubbles, which he saw as a fault (Champagne was a still wine in those days). Yet the good monk did devise a lot of viticultural and blending practices that are used to this day.

Then, as now, the Champagne region had very cold winters, and when fermenting wine gets too cold, the process pauses. Early Champagne-makers often thought their wine had finished fermenting and was ready to bottle, but it was actually lying dormant. Once the weather warmed up, fermentation continued: the remaining yeast reacted with the wine's unfermented sugar and created CO_2 in the sealed bottles, which built up until they exploded. Dom Pérignon figured out why this happened – but he was trying to stop it, not to encourage it.

Much of the wine from the Champagne region was exported to Britain during this time, where sparkliness was desirable. Legend has it a clever British chap worked out how to make a bottle sturdy enough to withstand the pressure – and Champagne as we know it was born. In any case, the traditional method not only produces a pleasurable sparkle, it adds flavour to the wine. After the second fermentation, a small amount of lees remains in the bottle to impart an 'autolytic' character: the yeasty flavour Champagne-lovers thirst after. It can be like toast, brioche, yeast or bread, but however you describe it, it adds complexity to the wine.

THE CHAMPAGNE
blend

Three main grape varieties are used to make Champagne: Chardonnay, Pinot Noir and Pinot Meunier. Each adds something to the blend. Chardonnay gives softness and fruitiness; Pinot Noir imparts structure and longevity; Pinot Meunier adds freshness and floral tones. In theory, a few other varieties, such as Pinot Blanc, are allowed in Champagne, but hardly anyone uses them any more.

Champagne styles and terms

VINTAGE

Made from fruit of a single harvest – the year is put on the bottle. The wine differs from year to year, depending on growing conditions. So, thanks to favourable weather, a 1996 will be full-bodied and concentrated; a '97 lighter in style; a '99 somewhere in between. Champagne houses only make vintage Champagnes in good years; the rest goes into their NV.

NON-VINTAGE (NV)

Champagne made mainly from fruit of one harvest, but with older wines added to make it taste the same as previous years. This 'house style' doesn't change. In theory, if you buy a NV Moët 'Brut Imperial', you'll know what to expect if you've had it before.

BLANC DE BLANCS

Literally 'white of whites': Champagne made only from Chardonnay grapes.

BLANC DE NOIRS

'White of blacks'. Almost all black grapes in Champagne are Pinot Noir or Pinot Meunier, so this basically means 'a pure Pinot Noir/Pinot Meunier Champagne' (normally pure Pinot Noir).

ZERO DOSAGE

The Champagne will be bone-dry. During production, a bit of sugar (*dosage*) is added to a bottle to keep it from tasting too dry, but if a wine is *zero dosage*, it hasn't had this little sweetener. The result is a bracing style that has marked acidity, and it can be eye-wateringly dry. Nice with oysters, though.

SEC/RICH/DOUX

Beware: this means 'sweet'! Not necessarily bad – it can be delicious – but worth knowing before you buy. Dry Champagne is *brut*. Weirdly, in Champagne terminology, *sec* (literally 'dry') means 'a bit sweet'.

THE TRUTH ABOUT
Champagne prices

Is Champagne worth it? In value terms, it's usually better to spend £25 on a bottle of, say, Aussie Chardonnay or white Burgundy than on cheap Champagne. But sometimes you've just got to have that *POP!* so remember that New World or Italian sparklers are often better value. If only the best will do, though, good Champagne remains the finest sparkling wine money can buy. Below are some brands usually seen in wine shops and restaurants. The ones with * I like, the ones with ** I love.

** Bollinger	* Charles Heidsieck	Lanson
** Pol Roger	* Deutz	Pommery
** Louis Roederer	* Veuve Clicquot	Mercier
** Billecart-Salmon	* Taittinger	Canard-Duchêne
** Jacquesson	* Perrier-Jouët	Piper Heidsieck
	* Moët et Chandon	
	* Mumm	

Thousands of smaller producers make wines every bit as good as the big houses, often with more character and better value. In fact, some of the big names buy in grapes, juice or even finished wine from contract growers, then sell it under their own labels. Many artisan producers, called *recoltant-manipulants*, carefully control the entire process, from growing grapes to the finished fizz; 'RM' will be on the label to let you know. These 'grower Champagnes' are well worth exploring.

SOME GOOD GROWER CHAMPAGNES
• Roses de Jeanne • Tarlant
• Jacques Selosse • Egly-Ouriet
• Varnier Fannière • Coutier
• Waris-Larmandier
• Lacroix • Bérèche

ROSÉ
If grape skins are left in when red grapes ferment, colour leaches out. Leave them a few weeks for red wine; take them out immediately for white. Leave them a day or two for a rosé. You can make good rosé Champagne this way, too, but Champagne is also the only region legally allowed to blend red wine into white to make a rosé style. Rosé Champagne can be amazing, but too often it's an excuse to cash in on 'lovers' who want pink fizz to guzzle before getting it on.

PRESTIGE CUVÉE
The best style or *cuvée* ('blend') a Champagne house makes, almost always vintage, but a pimped version. Louis Roederer's is 'Cristal'. Veuve Clicquot's is 'La Grande Dame'. They can be jaw-droppingly good, and it's the Champagne house's licence to print money. The difference between vintage and prestige fizz can be due to vineyards, cellaring treatments, aging practices, etc.

OTHER
sparkling wines

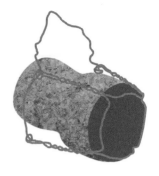

Cava

Cava is made in northern Spain via the traditional method, usually from Macabeo, Parellada and Xarel-lo grapes. Xarel-lo may sound like a planet in *Star Trek*, but its slightly smoky flavour adds interesting qualities to a Cava blend. If you taste a sparkling wine and it smells of burnt matches and rubber, chances are it's cheap Cava, but good Cava can be very enjoyable. A few big companies churn out the stuff at an amazing rate. They all make pretty reliable fizz, and compared to Champagne, it's cheap. There's a reason for this: even at the top, Cava rarely reaches the same level of complexity as good Champagne. Cava used to be called *Champaña* before the Champenois forced Spanish producers to change the name in 1970. This doesn't prevent Cava firms from using 'Champagne grapes', however, and Chardonnay and Pinot Noir turn up in Cava blends. You get all the same Champagne styles: non-vintage, vintage, rosé, *zero dosage*, etc. Don't worry about vintages here; all that matters is that Cava isn't too old. It's a fun drink to be enjoyed young.

SOME GOOD CAVA PRODUCERS
- Equipo Navajos
- Juvé y Camps • Parxet
- Segura Viudas

Prosecco

It's rare to find stunning Prosecco. It's very pleasant, but lacks the complexity of great sparklers. The best has good balance and attractive, perfumed, pear and apple aromas. Prosecco is made from the Glera grape in specified zones of Italy's Veneto and Friuli-Venezia Giulia regions. It comes in a variety of styles but rarely states which on the bottle; it's sometimes dry, sometimes off-dry or medium. Also, it can be as fizzy as Cava, or just lightly so. It's made via the tank method (see page 81) so doesn't have toasty, biscuity flavours. The best is DOCG Prosecco di Conegliano Valdobbiadene. The tiny subzone called Cartizze makes the very best of all.

Lambrusco

A fun, easy-going fizz from the Emilia-Romagna region, classic Lambrusco is a dry or off-dry red sparkling wine with high acidity (Lambrusco Reggiano tends to be sweeter), though you find white and rosé versions at various levels of sweetness and dryness. They make millions of gallons of the stuff every year. If you're looking for a sparkling red, you're probably better off with something from Australia, to be honest.

Other Old World sparklers

CRÉMANT from France is worth a sniff or two. It must be made with care to be called a *crémant*, particularly Crémant de Loire made from Chenin Blanc, or Crémant de Bourgogne from Chardonnay or Pinot Noir. Crémant d'Alsace has curiosity value, but Crémant de Bordeaux is rarely as interesting.

CLAIRETTE DE DIE TRADITION Made in a unique, old-fashioned way (like a simplified Champagne method), this bursts with sour-apple flavour and a nice bit of sweetness.

SEKT is made from Riesling. It's from Germany, and not exported as much as it once was. Give it a try, though, if it's called Deutscher Sekt; this tends to be fully dry.

MOSCATO D'ASTI from Italy's Piemonte region, is sweet, fizzy, peachy stuff, whereas normal Asti tastes more like nondescript cheap, sweet sparkling white. Both are made from Moscato, and are very low in alcohol (Asti around 8%, Moscato d'Asti 5.5%).

BRITISH SPARKING WINE Some of the UK's traditional-method wines are seriously good. Perhaps not always the best value, but for me there's something pleasing about enjoying a glass of genuinely good wine made in the UK that makes up for it.

MATEUS ROSÉ If it's subtlety you're after, it ain't Mateus. In its round, flat bottle; it's arguably the most well-known Portuguese wine: hugely popular in the 1980s, when it was responsible for 40% of the country's total wine exports. It still sells by the bucketload and is a medium-sweet, pink, fizzy drink.

New World sparklers

New World sparklers are often made via the tank method, so expect a fair bit of upfront fruit and flavour, if not always elegance and refinement as in Champagne. They tend to be a fair bit cheaper, and certainly have their place at a party. Sparkling wines are made in pretty much every New World country; the masters are the USA (specifically California) and Australia. Look for projects in warmer climes funded by the big Champagne houses, such as Moët's Green Point in Australia, or Roederer's Quartet in California. Both are made using the Champagne method and Champagne grapes, so they have those quintessential yeasty flavours and offer pretty good value compared to their French cousins. New Zealand does sparkling, too; a good example is the reliable and consistent Lindauer, or the Champagne-method Pelorus from Cloudy Bay, which is well-made and good value. I've also had good fizz from South Africa; look for *cap classique* on the label, This means it has been made using the Champagne method. South America concentrates more on still wines, but more and more of its sparkling wines are being exported – and many can be good value.

THE old WORLD

10

FRANCE

Print out a map of the world, cut out Australia and place it on top of Europe; it covers the entire continent. Yet the region of Bordeaux, France, produces more wine by volume than all the regions of Australia combined. That's how important France is.

When it comes to wine, France has more classic styles and fascinating regions than any other country. It can be confusing at times, but to get the most out of wine, you have to tackle France. Its dozens of small regions and tiny villages make fascinating and idiosyncratic wines, but for the purposes of this book, we'll concentrate on the six most important ones for still wine: Bordeaux, Burgundy, Rhône, Loire, Alsace and Languedoc-Roussillon.

BORDEAUX

At its best, Bordeaux is mighty and majestic. It is the land of grand *châteaux*; Château Lafite, Château Margaux, Château Latour. The best wines from these are held in the same esteem by some as the works of Victor Hugo, Matisse, Rodin. Bordeaux is wealthy and powerful; it makes more wine than any other region in France, and produces many of the world's most expensive. It's probably the most recognized wine region in the world, and is home to some of the most recognizable names in the world of wine. You can't deny that Bordeaux is a region of superlatives.

It also makes a fair load of overpriced rubbish that people buy just because the label says 'Bordeaux'. Yet Bordeaux is still worth exploring, but only if you're prepared to spend at least £15–£20 a bottle. The wines can be very enjoyable at this level if you choose carefully; above this and they can be breath-taking.

Bordeaux literally means 'next to waters', and that it is: just inland on the west coast of France, just past halfway down approaching the Pyrenees. A big river, the Gironde, runs through it, and it's a green and pleasant land, largely flat but for the odd low hill.

So what can you expect from a bottle of Bordeaux? Well, if red, typically something medium-bodied, with medium alcohol, medium tannins and medium acidity: a good benchmark in many ways. This list of 'mediums' is far from a list of 'averages', though; it's a sign of balanced wines. No wonder the British word for red Bordeaux, 'claret', is almost synonymous with 'wine' in the UK.

COMMON VARIETIES

RED
Cabernet Sauvignon, Merlot, Cabernet Franc

WHITE
Sauvignon Blanc, Sémillon

On the whole, red Bordeaux is made from a blend of Cabernet Sauvignon, Cabernet Franc and Merlot, although you occasionally see a smidgen of Petit Verdot, and you're technically allowed to use Malbec and Carmenère as well. The way it achieves this balance is often by using the three most common grape varieties – Cabernet Sauvignon, Cabernet Franc and Merlot – to complement each other.

Cabernet Sauvignon tends to be high in tannin, with good, strong acidity and pure black-fruit flavours. Merlot has less acidity, tannin and colour than Cabernet Sauvignon, but it does have a fleshy, silky character.

Merlot is the flesh; Cabernet is the bones. Together they make a perfect blend that provides a very balanced, complete wine.

Different *châteaux* make different wines out of these grape varieties, and each has its own blend. (By the way, in Bordeaux a *château* just means a wine estate – it doesn't always have a grand property on it).

Bordeaux does make a decent amount of white as well (about 25% of total production) and, again, it's all about the blend; this time mainly of Sauvignon Blanc, Sémillon and, less often, Muscadelle and a few other permitted varieties. Although the very best whites are sweet (Sauternes and Barsac), the dry whites can be excellent, too.

Because it's so big, the region of Bordeaux tends to be talked about in terms of 'left and right banks'. The river Gironde is, strictly speaking, an estuary that receives two rivers, the Dordogne and the Garonne, as they flow northwest towards the Atlantic. On the Left Bank of the estuary, closer to the sea, it's all about Cabernet Sauvignon; on the Right Bank, it's Merlot country.

Left Bank

Most of this part of Bordeaux is referred to as the Médoc, and is home to a number of famous subregions (or 'communes'): St-Estèphe, Paulliac, St-Julien and Margaux. From these come some of the most impressive, and most expensive, wines in the world. The reds tend to have higher proportions of Cabernet Sauvignon in the blend, and, as such, have a solid structure of tannin and acidity that helps them age. The very best can age for decades – the 1947s, for example, are still holding up well from a handful of top properties – and wines of certain *châteaux* will age a good deal longer than this. When it comes to typical flavour profile, a mature Left Bank Bordeaux usually offers some black-fruit aromas (particularly blackcurrant/blackberry), pencil shavings, cigar box; maybe some plum, chestnut or gamy aromas, too, as it ages.

To buy Bordeaux, you need to know its classification system: the *crus*. A *cru*, or 'growth', is the word for quality level in Bordeaux, so a first growth is the best in the scale, second growth is the next best and so on until fifth growths at the end. The list of designated *crus* is relatively short, and there are thousands of *châteaux* that don't appear on it, many of which are very good. The scale was created in 1855, when the leading *châteaux* of the day were ranked in order of quality according to the price they demanded at that time. This isn't a 'live' list, where contenders move up and down; it is set in stone (although Château Mouton-Rothschild moved up one to become one of the first growths in 1973; whether or not it deserves to be there is another question).

There are five *premiers crus*, or first growths: Château Mouton-Rothschild, Château Latour, Château Lafite-Rothschild, Château Margaux and Château Haut-Brion. The first three are in Paulliac, the fourth in Margaux and the last in Pessac-Léognan (south of the city of Bordeaux). There are 14 second growths (e.g. Château Léoville-las-Cases, and Château Montrose), 14 third growths (e.g. Château Giscours, and Château Lagrange), 10 fourth growths (e.g. Château Talbot, and Château Lafon-Rochet) and 18 fifth growths (e.g. Château Pontet-Canet, and Château Pedesclaux). If a wine comes from any of these, it's called *cru classé* or 'classed growth' Bordeaux.

Over the past 150 years, some *châteaux* have improved in quality and price and others have lost ground, so just because a *château* is a second growth doesn't mean it's better than all the third growths. Château Lynch-Bages, for example, may be 'only' a fifth growth, but its wines are consistently better than some fourth, third, and even second growths. That said, if the wine you're drinking is from a *château* found in the 1855 classification, it should be at the very least a decent wine.

The funny thing about Bordeaux is that, although the quality scale is unchanging, the estates are not.

They aren't defined in terms of vineyard area and they can buy and sell land as (and where) the *château* owner wishes. In Burgundy and many other regions, more emphasis is put on particular vineyards of fixed dimensions rather than on particular estates that can introduce grapes from new vineyards into their blends. This is one reason the wines of a particular *château* may get better or worse over time. Additionally, producers may have good winemakers or bad ones. And they may be lazy or passionate about quality.

Another quality level may be held by a Bordeaux *château* if it didn't make the *cru classé* scale, and that is *cru bourgeois*. There are 243 *châteaux* boasting this designation, and their wines can be a real bargain – for example, Château Cissac, Château le Boscq and Château Pontac-Lynch. There is also a breakaway group who have rejected the *cru bourgeois* classification and named themselves Les Exceptionnelles; most of these are also reliable, good-quality producers who don't charge ridiculous prices.

Underneath these, there are thousands of *châteaux* that don't hold any kind of official classification, but this isn't to say they aren't any good. The official legal wine classification structure in France is still the *appellation controllée/appellation protégée* system (see page 75), which is unconnected to the 1855 classification and still applies to all wine producers in Bordeaux. At the top, these are:

AC ST-ESTÈPHE Fairly full-bodied, solid wines that age well.
AC PAULLIAC The most consistently impressive commune; classic Bordeaux.
AC ST-JULIEN More classed growths than any other commune; prime vine-growing land. Gentle, nuanced, good quality.
AC MARGAUX Perfumed and seductive.

In the middle, there's AC Médoc. Again, there are some decent wines here at decent prices, but you have to know what you're buying.

At the bottom, you'll find AC Bordeaux and AC Bordeaux Supérieur. Don't expect much, but you might discover the odd decent glugger.

Right Bank

The wines of the Right Bank (or Libournais) differ from those of the Left Bank in a number of ways; most notably, they tend to have more Merlot and Cabernet Franc in their blends, making them more generous, rounded and softer in the mouth. 'Smoky plum' is the characteristic taste: rich and fleshy. More Merlot is grown here, partly because of the high proportion of clay in the soil – something the Merlot variety prefers. Cabernet Sauvignon, in contrast, feels more at home on the banks of gravel on the other side of the river.

The main region is St-Emilion, but, this being Bordeaux, the regions are then split up into loads of smaller subregions, just to make things complicated. They also decided to have a different, even more complicated, ranking system from the Left Bank – one-upmanship, if you ask me! But don't let it put you off, because these wines can be just as complex, subtle and nuanced as the wines from across the river.

In St-Emillion, the lowest rank for a *château* is *grand cru* and there are hundreds of them. Then there are the *grands crus classés* (57 of them), the *premiers grands crus classés* (15), and on top of this pyramid sit Château Cheval Blanc and Château Ausone in a mini class of their own: *premiers grands crus classés 'A'* (the rest of the *premiers grands crus classés* are rated '*B*'). This system is very different to the one over the river in that there is regular testing and the ability to move up and down rankings.

Pomerol lies next to St-Emilion and is a relatively small area, but it has some of the biggest names in Bordeaux. These wines tend to be softer and richer still than even St-Emilions. Pomerol doesn't have an official ranking system, but certain *châteaux* have better reputations than others. Pomerol is home to Château Pétrus, which, no one would contest, is the best wine in Pomerol, and possibly Bordeaux. It's certainly one of the most expensive: you're looking at around £1000 a bottle even for a poor vintage and twice, or even three times that, for a good one.

Other Bordeaux

A couple of other areas in Bordeaux deserve a mention.

ENTRE-DEUX-MERS (literally 'between two seas') lies between the Médoc and the Right Bank. This is not the most exciting of Bordeaux regions, but it's improving. A fair bit of decent dry white comes from here, and increasing amounts of respectable red.

GRAVES (pronounced *grahv*, referring to its gravelly soil) lies to the south of the town of Bordeaux itself and runs southeast. The wines from this region, both red and white, are improving all the time. The best part of Graves was given its own separate appellation, Pessac-Léognan, in 1987. The reds, typically Cabernet Sauvignon-based, tend to be medium-bodied, with a good concentration of fruit but no hard tannins. A bargain is hard to find in Bordeaux, but I've had a couple from Graves. If you're looking for good whites in Bordeaux, this is the best area to explore.

SOME GOOD VINTAGES 1900, 1914, 1921, 1929, 1945, 1947, 1953, 1959, 1961, 1966, 1982, 1985, 1989, 1990, 1995, 1996, 2000, 2005, 2009, 2010

AVOID 1980, 1984, 1987, 1991, 1992, 1993, 1997

SOME GOOD PRODUCERS
For a classic example of each of the main communes, you could do worse than the following (each will set you back £25–£35 a bottle): Château de Fieuzal in Pessac-Léognan; Château La Tour Figeac in St-Emilion; Château Chasse-Spleen in Moulis; Château Potensac in Listrac; Château La Tour-de-By in the Médoc; Château d'Angludet in Margaux; Château Lagrange in St-Julien; Château Croizet-Bages in Pauillac; Château Les Ormes-de-Pez in St-Estèphe.

BORDEAUX YEAR BY YEAR
Because of its marginal climate and the fact that it's subject to potentially dodgy weather, getting the right vintage is important in Bordeaux. It can make a big difference to the quality of the wine.

BURGUNDY

COMMON VARIETIES

RED
Pinot Noir, Gamay

WHITE
Chardonnay, Aligoté

If Bordeaux is to be admired, Burgundy is to fall in love with. There is something magical about these wines. A clever bloke once said, 'Quality is remembered long after the price is forgotten', and that's worth repeating to yourself when you see a good bottle on a restaurant wine list.

Like Bordeaux, Burgundy is not a region to explore unless you're willing to put your money where your mouth is – but my god, is it worth it.

Burgundy's wine production is very small in comparison to Bordeaux's, and demand outstrips supply, which hikes prices up. Be warned, though: a fair bit of shabby wine is made in this region, as producers know it will sell if it has 'Burgundy' on the label and it's relatively cheap. But for every average bottle, there's a work of art just waiting for you to uncork it.

Bourgogne Chardonnay

In the past few years there's been a movement in the press and among wine-drinkers called ABC, or 'Anything but Chardonnay'. Now I'm all for branching out and trying new things, but Chardonnay is still one of the greatest white grapes in existence, and Burgundian Chardonnay is a testament to what can be achieved with it. What they probably mean is 'Anything But Poorly Made, Over-Oaked, Aussie Chardonnay', and amen to that. But ruling out Chardonnay because of a few bad experiences is like ruling out eating beef after eating a few beef and tomato Pot Noodles (although to be fair that is the best flavour). And I'm sure they don't mean 'ABWB' or 'Anything but White Burgundy' as that would be madness, given white Burgundy is made from Chardonnay (apart from a tiny bit made from the OK, if somewhat plain, Aligoté grape, but it's always labelled as such).

Chardonnay from Burgundy can't really be summed up in a few words, but here are some broad descriptions. At the entry level of AC Bourgogne (which covers both Chardonnay and Pinot Noir), expect something medium-bodied, probably, but not always, with a hint (or more) of oak. It typically has some appley aromas and might be a touch floral. Moving up the quality scale into named villages wines, such as Rully or Mâcon, Puligny-Montrachet or Meursault, you should find a corresponding increase in complexity and nuance of flavour.

Chardonnay is actually a fairly neutral grape and the wine it creates depends a good deal on vineyard and winery practices, as well as individual sites (terroir). One thing you often find in white Burgundy is the use of oak barrels for the fermentation and maturation of wine. This tends to be more common with the more expensive examples, because only wines of pretty impressive character can stand up to the added flavours and influence of oak treatments, and oak barrels cost at least £500 each, so the price of using these will have to be factored into the selling price of the wine.

The two top tiers of the Burgundy quality classification are *premier cru* (i.e. famously good individual vineyards) and *grand cru* (the most famous and very best vineyards). These vineyards are essentially just patches of land with accepted boundaries. These can be jaw-droppingly expensive, but don't forget that the name of the producer is just as important. Sometimes you're better off buying the Bourgogne Chardonnay of a brilliant producer like Leroy or Leflaive than the Puligny-Montrachet of someone who isn't really trying.

Bourgogne Pinot Noir

You never hear anybody say they are 'ABPN' or 'Anything but Pinot Noir', which would make more sense than 'ABC' in some ways as it's a pain to grow and make reliably good wine from. On top of this, it's the most capricious of all grapes, and for every gorgeous bottle you open there'll be another one – in theory just as good – that won't be a pleasure to drink. It's almost as if individual bottles are prone to mood swings. And, if they don't want to play, nothing you can do will perk them up.

When conditions are right, however, Pinot Noir can produce some of the most magical wines of all.

Pinot Noir is the great red grape of Burgundy (you do also get some Gamay, but the majority is grown in Beaujolais, which we'll deal with separately later on). It likes clay and chalk, the two main soil types of the Burgundy wine region, which lies to the east of the centre of France. Typical aromas to expect in Pinot Noir from this region are strawberry, raspberry, beetroot, mushroom and farmyardy smells, and it's a great match for a lot of foods, particularly game, lamb and pork dishes.

It follows the same quality categories as white Burgundy: Bourgogne Pinot Noir; named villages such as Beaune, Pernand-Vergelesses, Gevrey-Chambertin; then *premiers crus* such as Beaune Teurons, Nuits-St-Georges Les St-Georges,

SOME GOOD PRODUCERS
Some bigger *négociant* (merchant wholesaler) houses like Bouchard, Jadot, Drouhin, Faiveley, Louis Latour and Chanson make average to very good wines, and tend to be reasonably safe bets.

The most exciting wines come from small-scale growers who often specialize in one tiny area. Some good ones who don't yet charge painfully high prices are Mark Haisma, Chandon de Briailles, Hudelot-Noellat, Hudelot-Baillet, Fourrier, Henri Gouges, Boyer-Martenot, Olivier Leflaive and de Montille.

If you go to someone's house and they pour one of these, get excited: Comte Georges de Vogüé, Domaine Dujac, Comtes Lafon, A. Gros, Armand Rousseau, Bonneau du Martray, Roumier, Leflaive, Sylvain Cathiard, Coche Dury, Leroy. At the top: Domaine de la Romanée Conti. The prices will make your eyes pop.

BURGU
Franc

and, finally, *grands crus* such as Gevrey-Chambertin 'Le Chambertin'. As an aside, this Burgundian village was once called just 'Gevrey', and is now 'Gevrey-Chambertin'; many villages of Burgundy have taken the name of their most famous vineyard and put it after their name. Like Vosne-Romanée after the *grand cru* La Romanée vineyard, and Chambolle-Musigny after the *grand cru* Musigny vineyard, etc.

Wines from these top-class vineyards become extremely complex, showing what's often described as an 'ethereal' quality. It can be moving to taste these wines, in the same way as looking at a beautiful landscape. There is something almost spiritual in their essence, something hypnotizing.

To live your life without sharing a great Burgundy with a good friend is more than a mistake; it is the very stuff of regret.

SOME GOOD VINTAGES 1990, 1995, 1997, 1999, 2002, 2005, 2006, 2009, 2010. Be wary of anything before 1985 for reds; Pinot Noir can age for longer but only the very best. Be careful of anything before 2002 for whites, as only the best can age much longer. For some unknown reason, even many of the top white Burgundies between 1996–2002 have aged badly and spoilt (a phenomenon known as premature oxidation, or 'premox').

AVOID Some decent Bourgogne Chardonnays and Bourgogne Pinot Noirs are available, but if you just want a good bottle of Pinot Noir or Chardonnay you're likely to find better value elsewhere.

Chablis

Chablis is officially part of the Burgundy region, but the area is much further north than the rest of Burgundy, and is treated as almost a separate entity. The grapes don't get as ripe, so the flavours of this white wine tend to be more at the 'green-apple' end of the fruitiness spectrum, rather than the riper, 'tropical' end. The law states that, to call itself a Chablis, the grape variety must be Chardonnay.

The quality levels work in the same way for Chablis as they do for Burgundy AC wines: i.e. at the bottom of the scale are wines named simply Chablis; then Chablis *premier cru*, and, at the top, Chablis grand cru. The *premier* and *grand cru* vineyards have fantastic, often slightly theatrical names like Grenouilles ('Frogs'), Beauroy ('Handsome King') and Vaudésir ('Desirable').

But, at the cheaper end, 'theatrical' is hardly a word you'd use to describe the wines of Chablis. The grapes retain their acidity and appley flavours and don't get too exuberant. One word you often come across when reading about Chablis is 'steely', which refers to its austere dryness and marked acidity. As you work your way up to *premier* and *grand cru,* the wines become more intense and full-bodied. Many top wines are aged in oak to add more texture and complexity. Dry white wines rarely age for that long in the grand scheme of things, but a *grand cru* Chablis should be happy to develop in the bottle for twenty years or so in a good vintage from a top producer.

P.S. It's perfect with oysters.

SOME GOOD VINTAGES 1990, 1992, 1995, 1996, 1997, 2000, 2002, 2005, 2007, 2010

SOME GOOD CHABLIS PRODUCERS
Vincent Dauvissat and Raveneau are amazing but expensive; Laroche, Pinson and William Fèvre are good. La Chablisienne is often a good choice. It's a cooperative: a company that buys the fruit of small, local growers, makes the wine and bottles it under the co-op's name – so it's not a *domaine*, or estate, like Dauvissat that grows its own fruit and makes its own wine.

Beaujolais

Beaujolais Nouveau has a lot to answer for. Thanks to the way it's made (a process called carbonic maceration) Beaujolais Nouveau can be bottled and drunk as soon as fermentation is finished, because this process produces a very light wine that doesn't require any aging to soften it. Tannins are fairly low, and the main point of most Beaujolais is to enjoy its young, fresh, fruity flavours.

It all started back in the 1950s, when a cunning Frenchman thought of a clever marketing ploy: bottle newly fermented wine as early as possible, create a big fuss and have a party to celebrate the new vintage.

Not that clever, actually, but it became a craze that eventually caught on in the UK in the 1970s, and has been celebrated globally ever since, on the third Thursday in November after the grape harvest.

But what folks back in the Seventies – the heyday of Beaujolais Nouveau – failed to notice was that, in the rush to get their wares out, the wines ended up not being that well made or interesting. Slowly people caught on, and began to think that perhaps Beaujolais was better avoided. But they were wrong!

Beaujolais Nouveau is indeed better avoided; 'normal' Beaujolais can be lovely. Although the Beaujolais region itself is technically situated in the much larger Burgundy region, Beaujolais wine doesn't have much in common with other red Burgundy. For a start, Beaujolais is made from Gamay – a variety rarely seen elsewhere. It makes light, pretty reds with a nice, high acidity, and without big tannins or much stuffing. Sometimes you don't want or need a big, gutsy red; you just want a red to go with grilled vegetables, or one that can be chilled on a summer's day. Beaujolais can fit the bill nicely at times like these.

Within the Beaujolais region there are ten villages (sometimes referred to as *crus*) which make more serious Beaujolais from their own distinct terroirs, and therefore these wines have their own distinct characters, each having earned their own AC as well. From north to south, they are:

ST-AMOUR Good light to medium in style.
JULIÉNAS Good quality on the whole. Tends to have a bit of structure
CHÉNAS The smallest, making fairly gutsy wines.
MOULIN-À-VENT One of the biggest Beaujolais styles; concentrated, long-lasting.
FLEURIE Typical Beaujolais: floral, not too light, but far from powerful.
CHIROUBLES Light and perfumed (and my favourite word in French).
MORGON Generally more powerful. Can be very good indeed and ages well.
REGNIÉ OK. Standard.
BROUILLY The largest Beaujolais AC region. Rarely exciting, but fairly robust and full-flavoured.
CÔTE DE BROUILLY Fuller in body and style than Brouilly.

Typically these wines are on the delicate side, and many people assume they don't age well. For lighter styles such as Chiroubles or Fleurie, that's correct, but the bigger styles can age for a good few years, and, in the best vintages, a Moulin-à-Vent can last for several, becoming more like its northern neighbours in Beaune and the rest of Burgundy as it matures.

SOME GOOD VINTAGES 1999, 2000, 2002, 2005, 2006, 2009.

SOME GOOD PRODUCERS
Foillard makes incredible wines; also Michel Tête, Château des Jacques, Domaine Marcel Lapierre, Georges Descombes and his son Damien Coquelet, and Domaine Lapalu. Not that his wines are that bad, but try and find growers other than the ubiquitous Georges Duboeuf (aka 'Mr Beaujolais'). If you're looking for a serious bottle of wine, you might want to avoid Beaujolais Nouveau altogether.

BURGUNDY
France

RHÔNE

The river Rhône rises in the Rhône Glacier in the Swiss Alps, then runs down via Lake Geneva into France. When it reaches Lyon, it joins its main tributary the Saône, then heads due south into the Rhône Valley before continuing down into the Mediterranean near Aix-en-Provence. The Rhône Valley is home to a diverse and fascinating wine country, from everyday quaffing stuff to some of France's finest red and white wines. There's really good value to be had here, right from the bottom up. Additionally, the Rhône tends to be more consistent than the other big wine regions of France. If you want to drink amazing wine without a sphincter-clenching price tag, the Rhône is worth a look. Conversely, if you want a cheap glugger with your spaghetti in front of the TV on a Tuesday night, it's also the region to turn to.

You've got to love the Rhône.

Like all the main wine-producing regions in France, the Rhône isn't just one area that makes similar wines. It is made up of two completely different regions: the northern Rhône and southern Rhône. To help you remember, the French call them *Rhône Septentrionale* and *Rhône Méridionale*. (Fortunately, you'll never need to know this...)

COMMON VARIETIES

RED
Syrah, Grenache, Mourvèdre

WHITE
Marsanne, Roussanne, Viognier, Grenache Blanc

- Most of the southern Rhône vineyards are planted on ancient riverbed. Most of the northern Rhône vineyards are planted on the slopes and hills on the banks of the river.

- The southern Rhône wine-growing area is a big circular swathe of land; the northern Rhône is a long, thin finger of land that tracks the river from north to south.

- Apart from Châteauneuf-du-Pape, most southern Rhône wines are gluggers to enjoy with a big grin of purple teeth. Apart from St-Péray, most northern Rhône wines are more brooding, tannic and impressive.

- Southern Rhône is Grenache Noir and Grenache Blanc country, alongside a massive host of supporting grapes. Northern Rhône reds are all 100% Syrah (except Côte-Rôtie, which can have up to 20% Viognier blended in). Northern Rhône whites are either Viognier, Marsanne or Roussanne. All are seriously interesting grapes, which is more that can be said for some of the random varieties they use in the south.

So, when it comes to choosing a bottle, don't lump all of the Rhône in one boat. South equals Grenache (warm, gutsy and broad); north equals Syrah (powerful, tannic and intense).

Southern Rhône
Châteauneuf-du-Pape, Gigondas, Vacqueyras, Rasteau, Côtes du Rhône-Villages and others

Many regions or countries are associated with one particular grape variety above all others. For the southern Rhône, this is Grenache: Grenache Noir for the reds and Grenache Blanc for the whites. But they don't just stop there; a bucketload of other local southern French varieties is chucked in for good measure.

Take Châteauneuf-du-Pape, the region's most famous appellation. It was the first AC set out in law in the 1920s to stop some random winemaker in Luxembourg calling his gut-rot the same name and charging a premium for it. But Châteauneuf has been famous for much longer than that. In the fourteenth century, the pope (*pape* in French) decided to move to Avignon and build a big new castle, or *château neuf* – hence the name. Like all good men of the cloth back then (when it comes to wine, we owe French monks a big debt of gratitude), he set up a big vineyard. When the monks tasted the results of said vineyard, they realized they were on to something.

Because delimiting (i.e. setting out by law) vineyard areas was a new thing in the 1920s, the regulations surrounding the Châteauneuf appellation are more detailed, complex, and just plain bonkers than any other French AC.

The laws stipulate that the vineyards of Châteauneuf may at no time be used for the landing of spaceships.

Somewhat unnecessary, perhaps, but not as unnecessary as permitting up to 13 possible grape varieties. (**GRENACHE NOIR**, **MOURVÈDRE**, **SYRAH**, **CINSAULT**, Muscardin, Vaccarèse, **PICPOUL**, Terret Noir, Counoise in red; **GRENACHE BLANC**, **CLAIRETTE**, **BOURBOULENC**, **ROUSSANNE** and Picardin in white, trivia fans. You're unlikely ever to come across the ones not in bold.)

Because of the number of varieties grown, and variable quality of producers, it's hard to generalize too much about the character of Châteauneuf-du-Pape, but on the whole, it's a medium- to full-bodied red, with fairly high alcohol and soft tannins (Grenache doesn't contain much tannin because this variety has thin skins, and skins are where much of the tannin comes from). The most important grape varieties in Châteauneuf are Grenache and Mourvèdre.

GRENACHE contains medium to low acidity, medium to low tannins, high alcohol and good body. It produces wines that are typically medium- to deep-coloured with plump, rounded strawberry fruit, sometimes with a herbal tinge.

MOURVÈDRE has medium acidity and full body, medium to high tannin and alcohol. Genius British wine-writer Andrew Jefford, describes it as 'gruff' and he's spot on. If any grape should have a beard, it's this one. It tastes of blackberries with a pleasant hint of compost, and sometimes with a faintly floral overtone (violets).

Whatever their exact blend, the wines of Châteauneuf can often be spicy, with cocoa, mocha and herb notes mixed in with cherry, strawberry and brambly fruit flavours. As they age, they often take on a pleasingly dank, farmyard aroma. They can be complex and expansively beautiful, but again, it's one of those well-known names – which means it can be a licence to print money for lazier producers of average wines.

You do also see a little white Châteauneuf on the shelves. They often used to be a bit rubbish, but they are improving on the whole. Examples from top producers can be excellent, but it takes a great winemaker to make something exciting out of Grenache Blanc. Be warned, though: white Châteauneauf doesn't age as well as the red stuff, so it's safest to drink it young rather than end up with a knackered bottle.

For the red Châteauneauf experience without paying papal prices, try a Gigondas. It's a village about 10km (six miles) northwest of Châteauneuf that makes similar wines, albeit more rustic. Next door to Gigondas is Vacqueyras, which makes an even more rough-round-the-edges version of Châteauneuf – but, with a bruiser of a dish like beef stew, you sometimes want something equally brutish but delicious to wash it down with.

Further down the scale of quality, but still with fantastic wines worth exploring, are the Côtes du Rhône-Villages wines, particularly those with a specific named village on the label such as Cairanne or Sablet, and also the appellation of Rasteau.

SOME GOOD PRODUCERS
Perrin, Château de Saint Cosme, Domaine la Soumade, Bernard Stehelin, Marcel Richaud, Domaine du Pesquier, Domaine de Fondrèche, Domaine de la Mordorée, Domaine du Vieux Télégraphe, Château de Beaucastel, Clos des Papes, Château Rayas

RHÔNE

France

Northern Rhône
(Crozes-Hermitage, St-Joseph, Cornas, Hermitage, Condrieu, Côte-Rôtie, St-Péray)

Syrah and Shiraz are the same: same grape, different name. It just goes to show how planting the same variety in a different place yields a completely different outcome. In Australia, it makes a full- to very-full-bodied wine with a deep, inky colour, high alcohol and intense fruit. French versions can be stonking wines, too, but in general, they're more restrained, balanced and less in-your-face. In the best years, these are stunningly beautiful wines. Sometimes winemakers in Australia call Shiraz 'Syrah', because they've purposefully made a northern-Rhône-style wine: a medium- to full-bodied red with a deep colour, fairly strong tannins and good acidity. They often have brambly, red- and black-fruit character, and a whiff of black pepper and crispy bacon about them.

The right whites

Northern Rhône whites can be equally impressive. To my mind, they fall into two camps: Roussanne and Marsanne vs. Viognier. Most northern Rhône whites are made from Roussanne and/or Marsanne; you find Viognier only right at the northern end of the valley, in Condrieu and Château Grillet.

Condrieu is surprisingly variable, both in style and quality, considering it's such a small appellation. Some wines are fresh, fruity and medium- to full-bodied, designed to be drunk young. Some spend time in oak, are fuller in body and built with aging in mind. Neither is necessarily better than the other. What unites the two is a perfumed, peach-and-apricot aroma and a surprisingly full body, with a heavy, almost oily mouth-feel. If any wine can be called buxom, it's this.

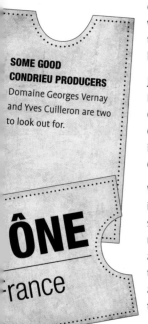

SOME GOOD CONDRIEU PRODUCERS
Domaine Georges Vernay and Yves Cuilleron are two to look out for.

Just south of Condrieu is one of France's tiniest appellations: Château Grillet. It was one of the very few ACs to be owned entirely by one family (the Neyret-Gachets) until it was bought up by François Pinault, owner of Bordeaux's Château Latour, in 2011. They make only about 10,000–13,000 bottles a year, and it's expensive. Château Grillet is a dry white made from Viognier; it's not unlike Condrieu, but it's leaner, and it can age for 20 years or more in a good vintage.

When it comes to Marsanne and Roussanne, the majority is dry. You'll know if it's sweet because it will probably come in a half-bottle, and it will make you sneeze when you see the price. The two grapes are similar, style-wise – kind of musky apricot, good medium to full body, and the best bottles sometimes have a herbal, celery-like finish. Roussanne is less full and a bit more muted but spicier than Marsanne; single-varietal Roussanne does exist, but it's more often used in a blend. Most Rhône whites from Marsanne and Roussanne aren't to everyone's taste – not like crowd-pleasing Chardonnay, say. They can be spellbinding, though.

Northern lights: from St-Joseph to Hermitage

The largest appellation in the northern Rhône is St-Joseph. Producers here certainly make a lot of disappointing wine, both in red and white. This is hardly surprising, given that the region covers about 650 hectares over a 40km/25-mile stretch of riverbank; not all of it is going to be good. But some wines from the best bits of the appellation can be outstanding – especially from vines growing on granite.

The next-biggest appellation is Crozes-Hermitage, the wider area that surrounds the smaller appellation of Hermitage. Anyway, reds here tend to be more interesting than whites, and they can be very good. It's unlikely they'll ever blow you away, mind, but Crozes-Hermitage can be a source of quintessential Rhône Syrah, with lots of black pepper, blackberry and spice notes. There's often decent value to be had here, even though the wines are rarely cheap.

All of the other appellations (Cornas, Côte-Rôtie, Hermitage) are very small, very exciting and very expensive. Cornas is the most rustic and just makes reds that age for decades and are austere and tannic. Cornas is Alan Rickman playing a baddy; don't mess with Cornas. As it gets older, it gets wonderfully stinky and animal-like.

Next up is Côte-Rôtie, another serious wine. It tends to be more complete and well-rounded, with a more perfumed aroma than lovely, dirty Cornas. Sometimes this is due to white Viognier: up to 20% is legally allowed in the blend. This practice has become fashionable in Australia, where more and more producers are making Shiraz-Viognier blends. Some are delicious, but most are not half as long-lived and complex as a Côte-Rôtie.

And, finally, Hermitage. Now this is the very pinnacle of the wines of the Rhône, in both red and white, the finest example of what is possible with Syrah (black fruits, minerals, meat, smoke, burnt fireworks) and Marsanne (apricots, peaches, musk, spice, celery, rhubarb).

These are wines of immense beauty and sophistication, and, compared to top Bordeaux, not insanely expensive.

SOME GOOD VINTAGES Getting the vintage right in the Rhône is easy but important. Since 1998 the northern and southern Rhône haven't had a bad vintage except 2002 – a total write-off due to dreadful wet weather. 2003, 2005, 2006, 2007 and 2009 are particularly good. In 2008, they weren't quite so lucky but the wines are still not bad among the better growers.

SOME GOOD ST-JOSEPH PRODUCERS If you're going to buy St-Joseph, know your producer. Gripa, Cuilleron and Gonon are reliable; their best bottlings are awe-inspiring and around £25 a pop.

SOME GOOD CROZES-HERMITAGE PRODUCERS One of the best is Alain Graillot, and Daniel Reynaud is also worth checking out. Jaboulet's Domaine de Thalabert can also be excellent.

SOME GOOD PRODUCERS For Cornas, look for Juge, Voge and Clape. For Côte-Rôtie, try Guigal, Jasmin and Rostaing, but Gilles Barge makes decent cheaper alternatives. Hermitage: Chapoutier is the boss and owns around a third of the hill of Hermitage. Jaboulet's La Chapelle is extraordinary in a good vintage. Domaine Jean-Louis Chave makes less, but is brilliant. His wines have huge complexity and can age for decades – that goes for red and white.

LOIRE

COMMON VARIETIES

RED
Cabernet Franc, Gamay, Pinot Noir

WHITE
Sauvignon Blanc, Melon de Bourgogne, Chenin Blanc

On the surface, with its gently rolling countryside, endless flowing river and agreeable towns, the Loire is a calm and rather unexciting place. Its *châteaux* are pretty. The region is perfectly pleasant. But once you get there, you begin to notice unusual details. Like the manicured lawns and Roman columns of the restaurant – hidden away in an industrial estate by the motorway. Then there's that hotel in a smart quarter of town – with the ebullient prostitutes at the end of the road.

The same goes for Loire wines. Much of the stuff that makes its way into UK supermarkets is uninspiring, passable or just approaching satisfactory. Explore a bit deeper, though, and, under the surface, you'll find gem after gem, in the most disparate styles. From just four main grapes, nearly every style of wine is made here.

The Loire is another of those French regions that's actually a number of different subregions under one name. The first is Muscadet, or the Pays Nantais, which lies at the mouth of the river Loire where it joins the sea halfway down the west coast of France. The river, which is the longest in France, reaches well into the east until it gets to the centre of the country, whence it heads south. 'Loire' wines are those grown along the west-east stretch. After the Muscadet subregion comes Anjou-Saumur, then the Touraine, then the Centre. Each has different specialities.

Pays Nantais: Good old Muscadet

The only wine you need to know about here is Muscadet. It's a simple but enduring French classic; it will never be an amazing wine to sit down and consider, but it does have a knack of hitting the spot perfectly with certain foods, refreshing you admirably in the process. Muscadet is made from a grape called Melon de Bourgogne, which is misleading as the grapes aren't from Bourgogne and, disappointingly, aren't as big as melons. But they do make a dry white that's high in acidity, without an awful lot else going on – which sometimes is just what you want. Furthermore, it goes brilliantly with fish. And it's as cheap as chips.

The wines from the appellation Muscadet de Sèvre-et-Maine are usually from better vineyards and have a tad more flavour. For more complexity, look for the words *sur lie* on the label. This means the wine was matured on its lees (the spent yeast cells from the fermenting process), which add flavour and a creamy texture. Don't worry about vintages where Muscadet's is concerned; just get the youngest wine you can find.

LOIRE

SOME GOOD PRODUCERS
Domaine les Hauts-Pémions and Château du Coing make decent ones.

Anjou-Saumur: a bit plain but with stonking stickies and quality reds

Most Anjou is better avoided. A lot of it is off-dry or medium rosé, cloying and dull. There are, however, some gems, made mostly from Chenin Blanc, one of the most versatile, underrated white grapes of all. It can produce dry wines, sweet wines, sticky dessert wines... even sparkling wines. It tends to have rich honey and quince flavours held together with a firm streak of acidity and a curiously agreeable whiff of wet dog, no matter what the style. In good years these wines can age for decades. But it's the sweet ones that captivate: thick, golden nectar with honey, flower, peach, mango and nut flavours. Good ones have underlying acidity and minerals that make you come back for more. Look for ACs Quarts-de-Chaume, Bonnezeaux and Coteaux du Layon. Some Saumur can be good: red from Cabernet Franc (particularly the Saumur-Champigny AC, which can make excellent light, silky reds with red-berry flavours: great chilled) and white from Chenin Blanc and Chardonnay.

SOME GOOD SAUMUR PRODUCERS For a good red Saumur-Champigny, try Domaine des Roches Neuves or Château de Villeneuve.

Touraine: Cabernet Franc, Chenin Blanc

Touraine is the home of red Loire. Look for two AC names: Chinon and Bourgueil (pronounced *borg-uh-ee*). Chinon is arguably the lighter, but both are fairly subtle reds. Both can also be delicious: fairly delicate in fruit intensity, body and alcohol but often with fine, smooth tannins, firm acidity and complexity. They frequently have blackcurrant aromas and a leafy, vegetal undertone.

Cabernet Franc is the skinny, brainy cousin to muscular, charismatic, if not terribly subtle, Cabernet Sauvignon. It can make satisfying wines, particularly in good vintages when the grapes ripen fully. In these instances, the best wines can age for 25 years, taking on intriguing aromas of pencil shavings as they do. Serve them cool, or chilled if you forget to take them out of the fridge in time.

Just down the road is Vouvray, where you'll find some pretty impressive whites made from Chenin Blanc. The sweetness level is stated on the label: from dry to sweet, it's *sec, sec tendre, demi-sec, moelleux, nectar*. If in doubt, ask. They tend to be honeyed, with a certain fruitiness. They can be anything from very dry, to off-dry, to medium, right through to fully sweet dessert wines, and even have different levels of fizziness. The sparklers can be very good, whether the slightly sparkling *pétillant* to full on *mousseux*.

SOME GOOD TOURAINE PRODUCERS In Chinon, Charles Joguet and Olga Raffault are brilliant. In Bourgueil, try Jacky Blot's Domaine de la Butte and Domaine du Bourg's St-Nicholas-de-Bourgueil.

SOME GOOD VOUVRAY PRODUCERS Marc Brédif makes some pretty good value bottlings. If you can find biodynamic wines made by Huet, snap them up. Vigneau-Chevreau makes a good sparkling.

SOME GOOD VINTAGES Ideally opt for the warmer years: 1996, 2000, 2002, 2005, 2009.

Centre: Sancerre and Pouilly-Fumé: amazing Sauvignon Blancs

Just as many people are familiar with Chablis but unaware it's made from Chardonnay, the same goes for Sancerre: it's the classic wine made from Sauvignon Blanc in France. As is Pouilly-Fumé, its less famous counterpart across the river. The white wines of Sancerre, at the far eastern end of the growing region of the Loire, are very much Sauvignon Blanc, but don't expect the pungent, gooseberry-and-kiwi-fruit New Zealand style here.

The Loire style is a lean, minerally expression of this grape, often with asparagus and freshly cut grass aromas.

This is, in part, due to France's cooler climate, but it's also due to the soil, which gives rise to two different styles. The first, grown on the local tufa soil (a kind of boiled chalk), is full and fruity; the second, grown on flint, yields a more gun-smoky, minerally version. As a rule, both will be very dry with high acidity, pale in colour, with medium body and medium alcohol.

You do occasionally also see rosé and red Sancerres, and these are made from Pinot Noir. Although some can be pale and interesting, they rarely have enough flavour to satisfy, except from top producers in warmer years.

Pouilly-Fumé (pronounced *POOey foo-MAY*) is very similar to Sancerre, but is a smaller appellation just down the road. It is a white-wine-only AC and it's not that easy to tell it apart from white Sancerre; both are made from Sauvignon Blanc in a similar style. As a rule of thumb, Pouilly-Fumé is marginally more full and rich than Sancerre, with less emphasis on steely acidity. Both are worth trying if you're fond of Sauvignon Blanc.

SOME GOOD VINTAGES Unless you're looking for one of the very best wines from this region, it's a good idea to stick to recent vintages; older than three years generally isn't a good thing for these wines, but top Sancerres and Pouilly-Fumés will last an extra year or two. In the best vintages, such as 2001, 2002, 2004, and 2005, wines from top producers will last much longer.

ALSACE

I know what you're thinking. It's the same as I once thought when I spotted wines from Alsace in the shops before my Alsace epiphany: 'Hmmm. Looks kind of interesting. But these bottles are tall and, well... Germanic-looking. Sounds a bit German, come to think of it. There could be something weird inside. And, to top it off, it's probably SWEET! I'd look like some kind of ignorant freak if I took this to dinner. Better go with the Jacob's Creek Chardonnay again.'

Years of my life wasted.

Alsace is one of the most interesting, rewarding and easy-to-understand wine areas in France, yet it's frequently avoided because it looks, well, Germanic – hence it's very good value. AND it makes you look like a genius when you take it to someone's place and it looks weird and German but tastes amazing.

Alsace is a region in northeastern France on the German border, tucked behind the Vosges Mountains. It has been fought over by France and Germany since the dawn of time: part of the reason for the split personality embodied in Alsace wine bottles and labels. Producers here also use some grape varieties that are more associated with Germany (Riesling, Gewurztraminer and, to a lesser extent, Pinot Blanc and Sylvaner), but also some that are more associated with Italy (Pinot Gris/Grigio) and France (Pinot Noir, Muscat). The wines are virtually always unblended, and labelled according to grape variety.

COMMON VARIETIES

RED
Pinot Noir

WHITE
Riesling, Gewurztraminer (spelled without the ü in France), Pinot Blanc, Pinot Gris, Muscat, Sylvaner

For clarity, Alsatian wines are not made by dogs, for dogs or made of fermented dogs.

One interesting way to approach grape varieties, however, is in terms of our furry friends. All dogs are the same species (*Canis lupus familiaris*), but there are lots of varieties; Golden Retrievers, Pugs, Great Danes, etc. All wines worth drinking are from the same species (*Vitis vinifera*) but there are lots of varieties; Chardonnay, Cabernet Sauvignon, Riesling, etc. In the same way that all dog breeds look different, all grape varieties taste different. And you can have lots of fun blending varieties together to slightly dodgy effect (Pinotage/Labradoodles).

You might assert that this is a stupid analogy, and you would be correct; but it's one I'm going to pursue when describing the grape varieties of Alsace. So turn the page...

TELLING SWEET FROM DRY
Most important of all to remember, unless it says *vendage tardive* ('late harvest') on the label (rare, sweet and rudely expensive), Alsace wines are usually DRY. Even the Muscats.

ALSACE

France

RIESLING (GREYHOUND)

Pronounced *REESE-ling*, this is undoubtedly one of the finest white grapes in existence, but it's often avoided by people due to its connection with Germany, where it is planted extensively. Thanks to increased experimentation with this grape in Australia and New Zealand, however, more people are trying it, and it's beginning to rise in popularity again. Riesling has a very precise flavour profile, marked by high acidity and a clean but assertive fruity flavour, typically of lemons, limes, satsumas, and often jasmine or sherbet. As it ages, it can take on an intriguing petrol aroma akin to overripe melons. In Alsace, it should be medium in body and alcohol, with medium to high acidity, usually dry, sometimes off-dry (particularly with the more expensive grand crus). When it comes to matching food, it goes well with salads, fish, pork and shellfish. It also has an amazing ability to age (particularly the sweeter German styles), hence the greyhound – it looks kind of weird to start with, but, once you get to know it, you can't help but love it. It's distinctive, and it will run and run and run.

GEWURZTRAMINER (POODLE, DYED PINK)

Gewurztraminer is even more distinctive than Riesling, possibly the most distinctive of all grape varieties. It is relatively low in acidity and has a highly perfumed and spicy aroma of lychees, roses and Turkish delight. It is a tart among wines. The alcohol level should be average, but it's fairly full-bodied and viscous in the mouth. The cheap stuff tastes like soap, but a good Gewurz should be more Dolly Parton than Britney Spears.

PINOT GRIS (LABRADOR)

Good old reliable Alsace Pinot Gris; it rarely lets you down. Not unlike a Riesling but with more weight and not quite so zippy in the acidity and flavour stakes. It typically shows peachy/apricot flavours in youth and should have high enough levels of acidity so as not to get flabby and overweight like a lazy Lab. It can age well, too.

MUSCAT (DACHSHUND)

You don't see a great deal of this on the shelves, but it can be interesting. It's the same grape as used for the sweet wines of the Rhône and Languedoc (see pages 99 and 110), but all the sugar has turned to alcohol. It typically has low to average alcohol levels, and is just about medium in body and acidity, but the interesting thing about Muscat is its perfumed nose, which actually smells and tastes of fresh green grapes. Like a Dachshund, a dry Muscat can be appealing in an almost 'cute' kind of a way – certainly distinctive, but not to everyone's taste.

PINOT BLANC (BEAGLE)

Unlikely ever to rock your world, nonetheless Pinot Blanc can be refreshing and, er, useful – like a Beagle. Medium in every respect, but largely lacking much in the way of any flavour. Which is actually sometimes what you want: just something to refresh the palate and help wash down a simple meal. The perfect match for a simple onion tart. Which says it all, really.

SYLVANER (NOVA SCOTIA DUCK TOLLING RETRIEVER)

An attractive name, but, in reality, not that interesting. Often a bit average and plain. Can be perfectly good in a slightly perfumed, floral, pleasant way. A bit like Pinot Blanc.

PINOT NOIR (WEIMARANER)

Alsace Pinot Noirs, the only reds from this region, are light in most respects, with lots of bright, red-berry fruit. They can be sleek and attractive, but, compared to Burgundy, they don't have the same intellectual qualities. Bit like a Weimaraner, really.

SOME GOOD PRODUCERS Hugel & Fils, F E Trimbach, Domaine Zind-Humbrecht, Domaine Weinbach, Domaine Marcel Deiss, Domaine Albert Mann, Domaine Marc Kreydenweiss, Domaine Paul Blanck, Domaines Schlumberger, Rolly Gassmann... So many great producers to explore.

LANGUEDOC-ROUSSILLON

The Languedoc-Roussillon is made up of two large areas that border each other, running from the middle of the southern Mediterranean coast to the border with Spain and stretching inland for 80km (50 miles) or so in a great swathe of hot countryside. This used to be peasant country, making a vast quantity of unremarkable plonk.

In the past 20 years, however, winemakers have taken a second look at the area and realized that, with a little TLC and by employing modern methods, some brilliant wines can be produced.

In some small pockets of land, exceptional wines are starting to make themselves known.

The Languedoc is an area made up of lots of little appellations, each with its own character and specialities. But, apart from the very top wines, you'd have to be a specialist to spot the difference between your average bottle of Faugères, Fitou, Corbières or Minervois. The majority of the region's wines are red and medium- to full-bodied, with medium to high alcohol and often intense fruit flavours.

They are frequently described as 'rustic' – that is to say, not as refined and sophisticated as, say, the wines of Bordeaux, perhaps with less-than-perfect balance, or with rougher tannins (but by no means unenjoyable). Often the reds from this area are a blend of a number of grapes, typically a fair whack of Grenache, a splash of Cinsaut/Cinsault, a dollop of Syrah if you're lucky, a vat of Carignan if you're not (it takes a skilled winemaker to make a great wine from Carignan).

When it comes to most of the more everyday reds from this area (which is about 99% of what's produced), don't worry too much about the year on the bottle; just drink it within four to five years of vintage. Most are meant to be drunk pretty much immediately anyway. Drink the dry whites straight away, and anything older than three years is probably too old.

Not that you see much dry white from this area; it's too hot and the grapes they use (Grenache Blanc, Bourboulenc, Rolle, other local varieties) don't take to long aging. Do look for Picpoul de Pinet, though, which is a very dry, lemony white from the Picpoul Blanc grape (Picpoul means 'lip stinger' in the local dialect and it's no lie), which is often great value.

When it comes to sweet whites, a great deal of Muscat is made in these parts, much of which is of a decent quality and decent value.

If you're looking for a simple sweetie to pimp your dessert course but don't want to spend more than a fiver on a half-bottle, you should be able to do it with a decent Muscat de Frontignan or Muscat de Rivesaltes.

Another one that deserves a mention is a sweet red wine called Banyuls, which is made in the area of the same name close to the Pyrenees. It's not unlike Port, but is less refined and takes on a pleasingly rustic, caramel flavour as it ages (it can last for decades). Banyuls goes well with chocolate, which is tricky to match with wine. Sniff it out.

Finally, an honourable mention goes to the appellation of La Clape, for sounding like a disease.

The wines can be great, though, particularly those of Château de la Negly; Château de Capitoul is good as well.

One Languedoc producer that is definitely worth the money is Mas de Daumas Gassac, near Montpeyroux (the white is impressive, the red can be utterly brilliant). Not in an appellation, its wines are simply classed as IGPs (*Indication Géographique Protégée Pays*, the replacement for *vin de pays*; see page 75), because they contain some non-traditional grape varieties. Currently listed at around £25–£30 a bottle, they ain't cheap, but they are worth it.

Lots of other IGPs from this region are closer to the £7 mark, however, and are often good value. Frequently made from a single grape variety stated on the bottle, they're often more New World in style than a lot of the more stubbornly traditional French wine styles.

SOME GOOD LANGUEDOC-ROUSSILLON PRODUCERS
Domaine de Montcalmès,
Château d'Aussières,
Domaine de l'Aigle,
Domaine Coudoulet,
Mas de la Séranne

LANGUEDOC-ROUSSILLON
France

11

SPAIN

C onsidering France and Spain are nearly the same size, it's surprising to learn that Spain has much less variety in its wines. This is due mostly to the fact that it's so intensely hot and dry there. That said, in many ways, Spain is more exciting. With the injection of modern winemaking methods and a new thirst for quality, more of its previously average-plonk-producing areas are suddenly making some outstanding wines. Since they're still finding their feet and don't yet have a big reputation, many also offer good value for money.

Not all grape varieties are created equal: a fact that's clearly illustrated in areas such as Alsace (see page 107). A lot of the quality wines from Spain are produced from one Spanish grape: Tempranillo (pronounced *tem-pran-EEo*). It has loads of pseudonyms in Spain (Ull de Llebre, Cencibel, Tinto Fino, Tinta de Toro...), but is most likely to be listed as 'Tempranillo' on a label. This variety is every bit as good as any other red grape, but it seems to prefer residing in this part of the world – unlike, say, Cabernet Sauvignon, which is at home almost everywhere.

Wines made from Tempranillo are typically medium- to full-bodied, with medium to high acidity, firm tannins, red or black berry-fruit character, and sometimes with a hint of leather or roses. At its best, Tempranillo can make wines of tremendous complexity and extraordinary longevity.

Historically, the white wines of Spain have been somewhat plain and sometimes not terribly well made. They're most commonly made from Airèn or Viura, varieties that are easy to grow and drought-resistant, but they don't taste of much. However, this is changing, and a number of interesting whites are cropping up, particularly in northwestern Spain.

The Spanish wine most people are familiar with is Cava: a cheap, but often decent-value, sparkling wine from the northeast; this is covered in the section devoted to sparkling wines on page 84 of this book.

COMMON VARIETIES

RED
Tempranillo, Garnacha (Grenache), Graciano, Mazuelo (Carignan)

WHITE
Airen, Viura, Malvasia, Verdejo, Albariño

RIOJA

One of the greatest, and certainly the best-known expression of Tempranillo is Rioja, made in a region that runs along the Río (River) Oja (hence the name) in the far north of Spain near the Pyrenees. The red wines from this region can be made from a blend of up to four varieties: Tempranillo, Garnacha, Graciano and Mazuelo.

Garnacha is the other grape variety that crops up all over the place in Spain, and it's the same grape the French call Grenache (see Southern Rhône, page 100), so it adds a fullness, body and warmth to the sometimes-uptight Tempranillo, padding it out in the same way that Merlot fills out and softens Cabernet Sauvignon in Bordeaux. Mazuelo is the French Carignan grape (see Languedoc, page 110) in Spain it's also sometimes called Cariñena. Graciano is a variety you won't see anywhere else, and there isn't even that much grown in Rioja because it's a tricky blighter to work with. Graciano is most often blended with the other permitted Rioja varieties, but on its own it can be spicily intense and delicious.

Tempranillo has a real affinity with barrel-aging, and in Rioja there are varying levels of oak use. The basic rule is that the better the vintage, the longer the wine can spend in oak. There are four levels.

IOJA

Span

SOME GOOD RIOJA PRODUCERS
López de Heredia, CVNE, Marqués de Riscal, Viñedos del Contino, Bodegas Roda, Bodegas La Rioja Alta, Bodegas LAN, Bodegas Muga. Marqués de Cáceres and Bodegas Navajas are reliable at the cheaper end.

1 **JOVEN** No oak aging, for early drinking.

2 **CRIANZA** Minimum one year in oak barrels and one year in bottle before sale.

3 **RESERVA** Minimum one year in oak barrels and two years in bottle.

4 **GRAN RESERVA** Minimum two years in oak barrels and three years in bottle. Only wines from the best vintages will be capable of long-term aging like this.

But, just because you see a term on a label doesn't necessarily guarantee quality; the producer is as important as ever. Equally, an increasing number of modern producers make brilliant Rioja, but they don't want so much oak influence in their wines, so, although their wines are excellent and can age well, they don't get considered for the *gran reserva* category.

These terms are also used elsewhere in Spain and Portugal, with slightly varying times in cask and bottle, but the general idea is the same.

The same terms are applied to white Rioja, but with less time required in bottle and barrel for each category. White Rioja is a real 'Marmite wine': you either love it or hate it. It's made from Malvasia and Viura, usually a blend of the two, and sometimes with Garnacha Blanco; Verdejo (see Rueda) is also legally allowed in the blend in a DOCa Rioja (see Grading System, page 75), and so are the ubiquitous Chardonnay and Sauvignon Blanc (but not that much, percentage-wise). White Rioja tends to be very dry, with moderately high body and alcohol, but without much fruit flavour, showing more nutty, vanilla flavours from the oak, especially the *gran reservas*, which can be very savoury and complex.

SOME GOOD VINTAGES Vintages do make a fair bit of difference in Rioja, but, apart from here and Ribera del Duero, don't worry about them too much. The ones below shouldn't let you down.

1989, 1990, 1991, 1994, 1995, 1996, 1999, 2001, 2004, 2005. 2002 was less successful.

NAVARRA

If you like Rioja and fancy branching out, the little region next door to the east, Navarra, is worth a quick look, too. It has a lot in common with Rioja, and uses very similar grape varieties, but its wines rarely get as amazing at the top end. However, they tend to be cheaper at the more everyday level, and are often a source of good-value bottles, particularly if you like rosé.

NAVARRA
Spain

SOME GOOD NAVARRA PRODUCERS
Bodegas Ochoa, Emilio Valerio

CATALUNYA

Catalunya (Catalonia to English-speakers) is a fascinating, modern and forward-looking region in many ways, not least when it comes to wine. It is located in the far northeastern corner of Spain, at the foot of the Pyrenees along the Mediterranean coast, with Barcelona at its heart. This area is best known as Cava country (see Sparkling Wines, page 86), but there's also a good deal of still wine produced across a number of *denominacións de origem* (DOs; see Grading System, page 77), most important of which are DO Penedès and DO Priorat. The two are at different ends of the scale.

> *Penedès makes lakes of everyday wines (and some excellent fine wines), whereas Priorat makes tiny amounts of top-class fine wines.*

You can't talk about Penedès without mentioning Miguel Torres, the most important producer in Spain, which creates vast quantities of wine. You might be familiar with Torres' Sangre de Toro, Coronas and Viña Sol brands that can be found throughout the UK, Spain, and in many countries around the world. When it comes to big wine brands, most of them should be punished for crimes against pleasure. Yet, although they're undoubtedly commercial, the Torres wines are good-quality and fairly priced – despite the company's large sales volumes.

Quite what made anyone grow vines in Priorat I'll never know. It's like trying to grow them on a blackboard on Mars. The ground is pretty much solid quartz, with a topsoil of quartz shingle and dust. It's so hot that your eyes start to pop out of your head – like Arnold Schwarzenegger's in *Total Recall*. Then, of all things, producers here decided to plant Carignan, that most unwashed of grape varieties. Fortunately they planted Grenache as well. A lot of vines die, but those that do make it yield highly concentrated, intensely flavoured wines with full body and punchy alcohol levels.

Interest in Priorat started in the 1980s; by the 1990s, its wines were being hailed as some of the best in the world. Because of the hype and the very difficult growing conditions, prices shot sky-high. It's possible to find cheaper examples now that are worth drinking, but you'll be hard-pressed to get a good one for less than £20.

PENEDÈS
Cheaper, commercial, often well-made wines

PRIORAT
Makes top-class fine wines, but at fairly astronomical prices.

CATALUNYA
Spain

RIBERA DEL DUERO

The Duero in western Spain is the same river that cuts east-west through northern Portugal, where it is known as the Douro. Although this area doesn't have the same heritage and recognition as Rioja (yet), Ribera del Duero is Spain's other important red-wine-producing region, and at the top end, it actually commands higher prices for its full-bodied, powerful and polished reds.

This is thanks mainly to a single producer, Vega Sicilia, which has been making one of Spain's best red wines for over a hundred years. It brought in Cabernet Sauvignon, Merlot and Malbec from France, and these grape varieties have acclimatized nicely to this high-altitude region, adding extra complexity and guts to the local Tempranillo, known here as Tinto Fino.

Vega Sicilia has since inspired several other local winemakers to make something a little more interesting than the plonk this area churned out for generations. Today, the region includes almost 250 wineries, and that number seems set to expand, although style and quality have been called inconsistent.

Nonetheless, more and more ambitious producers are springing up today in Ribera del Duero, and more and more great wine is being produced here.

RIBERA DEL DUERO
Spain

SOME GOOD RIBERA PRODUCERS
Alejandro Fernandez, Alión, Dominio de Pingus (if you're feeling minted)

ALSO TRY...
PSI, Bodegas Los Astrales, Bodegas Briego –all at the cheaper end of the scale

RUEDA

One of the few areas in Spain that produces exciting whites. Rueda, to the west of Ribera, on the northern border with Portugal, specializes in the Verdejo grape, which makes a dry white with decent acidity levels and some interesting tangy fruit flavour to back it up. It's often blended with the more boring Viura. Marqués de Riscal does a decent inexpensive example. You can also find some good cheap Sauvignon Blancs from this area that are worth a try.

LA MANCHA

An endless dustbowl in the centre of Spain. There are a few producers of some quality starting to crop up now, but, on the whole, unless you get a reliable recommendation, the wines here are likely to be either plain whites or moody reds.

VALDEPEÑAS

Valdepeñas is an area on the southern border of La Mancha, but it tends to make better wines that its northerly neighbour. Most of the better reds are produced from Tempranillo, and winemakers sometimes use oak-aging (like Rioja) to *crianza*, *reserva* or *gran reserva* levels. The results can be good, and much cheaper than Rioja at the higher levels of aging, but the wines tend not to be as complex or interesting, and the flavours, although big and ripe, sometimes get a bit muddled and lose their definition. At present, some good-value reds are being produced; with more investment and better winemaking techniques, though, Valdepeñas could do even better.

JEDA
MANCHA
Spain

VALDEPEÑAS
Spain

There is one area in particular outside of Rioja that is making excellent, world-class white wines, and that area is Galicia, in the very northwest of Spain. This region is totally unlike the dusty, baking central parts, thanks to all the rain coming in off the Atlantic. Galicia is one of the wettest regions in Europe, in fact, but it also enjoys lots of sunshine.

The grape to look for here is the Albariño, which has been making a comeback over the past 15 years or so.

SOME GOOD PRODUCERS
Palacio de Fefiñanes,
Paco & Lola and
Bodegas Terras Gauda

I've yet to find anybody who doesn't like Albariño; it makes a delicious medium-weight white wine with relatively high acidity and alcohol levels and lip-smacking zesty, aromatic fruit flavours.

On the whole, Albariño is best drunk young, but it shouldn't be knackered two to three years after the vintage. It can make a fine alternative to Sauvignon Blanc when you want something refreshing but don't feel like a grassy/asparagus/kiwi/gooseberry flavour that can be a bit insistent and attention-seeking if you're not in the mood. Goes well with seafood.

12

ITALY

F or much of its history, Italy remained a collection of autonomous states rather than a unified country, a condition made all the easier by its mountainous terrain. These geographically diverse regions thus evolved independently from each other with strong local identities. It's against the same background that the wine and food of each region developed, both separately and regionally.

All of Italy's winemaking regions are quite distinct from each other, and each has a good number of indigenous grape varieties. They seem to have an authenticity manifested in loads of quirky, wonderfully imperfect wines that go fabulously with food – and indeed, sometimes they're hard to get your head (or tongue) around unless you've got some food on hand at the time. As such, many of these wines aren't always as well-suited to drinking on the sofa with a friend in front of the TV as some easy-to-please Aussie bottles. So we'll concentrate on the classic wines you're likely to come across on a day-to-day basis, then look at a few grape varieties that are becoming increasingly prominent and widespread.

COMMON VARIETIES

RED
Nebbiolo, Merlot, Cabernet Sauvignon, Sangiovese, Nero d'Avola, Negroamaro, Primitivo, Aglianico, Montepulciano, Barbera, Dolcetto, Corvina

WHITE
Trebbiano, Garganega, Malvasia, Verdicchio, Fiano

TOSCANA/TUSCANY

Out of Italy's 23 designated wine-producing regions, three are the most exciting and are also home to the most commonly seen Italian wines outside of the country. The first of these is Toscana (Tuscany), located almost halfway down the 'boot'. This is the birthplace of a number of really classic wines, the most famous of which is **CHIANTI**.

TUSCAN WINE STYLES
Chianti, Vino Nobile de Montepulciano, Brunello di Montalcino (Sangiovese), Super Tuscans

Chianti is one of Italy's most celebrated red wines, but, as much as it reaches skyward, it also can plumb the depths. To ensure you get hold of a quality bottle, look for the words Chianti Classico on the label (there's a purple sticker with a black cockerel on it); this means that this particular Chianti has been produced within a designated high-quality area and made with more stringent laws governing viticulture and vinification than a wine not bearing that designation. There are a number of subzones in Chianti, and one worth seeking out is Chianti Rufina.

Sangiovese (pronounced *san-gio-VAY-sie*) is the most widely planted red grape in Italy. On the whole, it's rather pale in colour and medium-bodied, with medium

alcohol. Tannin can be fairly pronounced and noticeable, and you'll often get fairly high acidity in the wine. When it comes to typical flavours, expect red cherry, redcurrant and perhaps violets and almonds. Sangiovese can make remarkable, long-lived wines, particularly when planted in its Tuscan homeland. Because of its high tannin and acidity, it's ideal as a food wine, the perfect match being some fava beans and a man's liver – Hannibal Lecter's food and wine matching skills were spot on. Seriously, though, if you like a bit of offal, particularly liver, then Chianti can be a good choice (fava beans, by the way, are the same as broad beans in the UK).

Chianti Classico can be made just of Sangiovese, or it can contain small amounts of international varieties, such as Cabernet Sauvignon, Syrah and Merlot, alongside other traditional blending varieties of Canaiolo, Colorino, Malvasia and Mammolo.

CHIANTI VINTAGES Anything from 1997 onwards is pretty good, but avoid 2002. 2004 and 2006 were particularly good.

Italy used to have some notoriously nonsensical wine laws, and it was partly a rebellion against these that gave rise to experimentation with international varieties in the 1960s and '70s. This, in turn, was responsible for creating some of Tuscany's most notable wines, dubbed **'SUPER TUSCANS'**. These are wines made by certain maverick producers who wanted to experiment with international grape varieties such as Cabernet Sauvignon and Merlot using modern winemaking techniques.

Because they didn't comply with local wine laws, the wines were downgraded from the DOC or DOCG quality level to *vino da tavola* (table wines) – the level normally reserved for the most basic plonk. The difference, of course, is that these were – and still are – some of the most exciting and extraordinary wines Italy has ever produced. The 'downgrading' has since been remedied by the creation of the *indicazione geografica tipica* (IGT, or 'geographic indication of type') category, which has a very good reputation for quality.

SOME GOOD SUPER TUSCAN PRODUCERS
There are several names to look for: Sassicaia, Tignanello, Masseto, Solaia and Ornellaia are the most famous – hugely expensive but unforgettable.

The other style of blended Tuscan Sangiovese is **VINO NOBILE DE MONTEPULCIANO** (not to be confused with Montepulciano d'Abruzzo, which we'll look at later). Like Chianti, this was made traditionally from a blend of Sangiovese, Canaiolo, Trebbiano and Malvasia, although it now more commonly uses 100% Sangiovese. More full-bodied and alcoholic than Chianti as a rule, it displays deep, savoury flavours and can be superb.

One Tuscan wine is always made from pure Sangiovese. **BRUNELLO DI MONTALCINO** is similar to Chianti In many ways, but with three vital differences. The first is that, although made from the Sangiovese grape, it's a particular strain (or 'clone') called 'Brunello'. The second difference is that it's made in a warmer, drier region than Chianti. The third is that these wines are aged for at least three-and-a-half years in oak barrels. All three factors make for a full-bodied, intense, alcoholic and long-lived wine. This wine style is unusual in that it was effectively invented by one estate, Biondi-Santi, but was then copied by many others in the area.

SOME GOOD BRUNELLO DI MONTALCINO PRODUCERS
The Biondi-Santi family continues to make extraordinary wines, but also try Argiano, Tenuta Il Poggione, Collemattoni and Poggio San Polo for more representative examples.

BRUNELLO VINTAGES Anything from 1995 onwards is pretty good, but avoid 2002. 2004 and 2006 were particularly good.

PIEMONTE/PIEDMONT

While most of Tuscany's wines are blends, Piemonte (or Piedmont) usually produces wine from single grape varieties. In Tuscany, Sangiovese is king, but in Piemonte it's Nebbiolo that produces the best wines. This is the grape that makes **BAROLO** and **BARBARESCO**, the king and queen of this region. In some ways, these wines are reminiscent of top Burgundies: both have a complex, woodland character and can be hauntingly beautiful.

The Nebbiolo grape produces medium- to full-bodied wines with very high tannin, high acidity and medium to high alcohol, often with aromas of tar, roses and earthy truffles over its plummy fruit flavours. Barolo tends to be viewed as the more full-bodied choice, with Barbaresco the slightly softer style. Both are wines to fall in love with (or over).

PIEMONTESE VINTAGES
Anything from 1995 onwards, avoiding 2002 if possible.

A number of smaller regions around Piemonte grow Nebbiolo, which is sometimes known locally as Spanna. Although they rarely reach the heights of a good Barolo, they can be a cheaper way to find out what the grape is all about. **ROERO** and **GATTINARA** are good examples; the Langhe hills, in central Piemonte, are where these are situated, and **LANGHE NEBBIOLO** can often be a good bet from a good Barolo or Barbaresco producer.

Another couple of red grape varieties that are important to this region are Barbera and Dolcetto.

Although less prodigious, Barbera is much more common than Nebbiolo in Piemonte, because it is much easier to produce. It's most commonly seen labelled as **BARBERA D'ASTI** or **BARBERA D'ALBA** (two of the biggest production zones for this variety) and can be good, but some can appear out of balance if you don't drink them with food to temper their high natural acidity levels and more moderate levels of tannin and alcohol. When well made, however, these can make an enjoyable glass of bright, smooth, cherry-flavoured wine that goes particularly well with sausages.

Dolcetto, again often seen labelled as **DOLCETTO D'ALBA**, is not unlike Barbera in as much as it can seem out of balance in cheaper bottles, but shows better with food. In many ways, it is the inverse of Barbera: instead of high acidity and low tannins, it has less acidity and more tannin, and is typically soft and fragrant. Less interesting than Barbera and Nebbiolo, though.

Piemonte is also home to an important still white wine. **GAVI** (or Gavi di Gavi, grown near the town of Gavi) was very fashionable in the 1970s, but then started resting on its laurels and the quality went downhill. Because of this, it has had to drop its prices, and it can be better value these days, though it's still not cheap compared to many Italian whites. Gavi is made from Cortese: a relatively neutral grape that tends to be fairly subtle, with pear and almond aromas and a lemony finish.

SOME GOOD PIEMONTESE PRODUCERS
If you're feeling flush, try: Aldo Conterno, Paulo Scavino, Luigi Scavino, Luciano Sandrone, Elio Altare, G Conterno, Marchesi di Gresy, La Spinetta, Bruno Giacosa, Pio Cesare, Vietti. Slightly cheaper but still very good are Giuseppe Rinaldi, Brezza and Produttori del Barbaresco.

PIEDMONT
Italy

VENETO

VENETO

WINE STYLES
Valpolicella, Soave
and Bardolino

Veneto is the area just inland from the coast around Venice in northeast Italy, and it is an area blessed with a number of classic wine styles, including Valpolicella, Bardolino and Soave. You've probably seen them on supermarket shelves or wine lists at some point. What do they have in common? Not much, really, apart from the fact that there are a lot of boring (or just plain bad) versions of each out there. Equally, though, there are good-quality examples around if you look hard enough.

Valpolicella and Bardolino

Valpolicella and Bardolino are both light-bodied, dry reds with high acidity and reasonably high tannin. They tend to lie at the lighter, Loire reds/Beaujolais end of the body/intensity scale, although some producers make bigger, more concentrated versions. Both are made principally from the Corvina grape, with some Rondinella and Molinara blended in (though you'll probably never see these varieties on labels).

This is another example of the genius of Italian wine laws: Corvina makes decent wine, but Rondinella and Molinara are both pretty rubbish, yet they must make up at least 30% of the blend legally to be classed as a DOC Valpolicella. Fortunately, many producers simply ignore this nonsense and miss out the ugly sisters. Two clues on the label point to the good bottles:

1 **CLASSICO** This means the wine is from the best growing area.

2 **SUPERIORE** This means it has a higher (although still just medium) level of alcohol and has been aged for a year before release.

SOME GOOD VALPOLICELLA PRODUCERS
Masi, Prà Morandina, Tommaso Bussola, Zenato and Allegrini all make great examples.

VENETO
Italy

Bardolino uses even less Corvina in its blend, but Valpolicella is definitely the better of the two styles. Three variations of Valpolicella are worth sniffing out:

1 **AMARONE** Essentially this is a Valpolicella made from superior bunches of grapes that have been dried in racks before being crushed and fermented. The wine is then aged in oak barrels. Some of the grapes may be affected by a disease called 'botrytis' aka 'noble rot', depending on the winemaking style. This sounds dreadful, but actually all the fungus does is suck the water out of the grape, thus concentrating all the sugar, acidity, flavour and body components. Typically, Amarone is a full-bodied, concentrated red with high alcohol and deep, complex flavours – and it's DRY.

2 **RECIOTO** Made by the same method as Amarone, but this wine is SWEET.

3 **RIPASSO** To beef up their Valpol, producers sometimes chuck in some of the unpressed skins left from their Amarone into the tanks to add flavour, tannin and alcohol. This creates a kind of Valpol on steroids.

Soave

Whenever I suggest a Soave, people often seem nonplussed, but I'm finding more and more good, interesting Soaves all the time. It's fast becoming one of my favourite Italian whites, especially when it comes to getting value for money. However, they make enough Soave to fill an aircraft hanger every 30 seconds* (*approximate figure) so a fair bit of it is likely to be rubbish.

Good Soave has medium acidity with a hint of white peach and a nice bitter twist on the finish. It's made from the Garganega grape, since you were asking. If you see one by Inama or Pieropan, buy it.

A FEW OTHER ITALIAN
wine styles

1. *Frascati*

If you've been to a pizza/pasta place in the UK or USA, you've seen Frascati on the wine list. This probably ought to change. OK, so it's not that offensive, but Frascati is hardly the most exciting Italian wine out there. It's made just outside Rome in the Lazio region, and you often see it in those ugly squat bottles (this is an omen). Frascati is made from Trebbiano and Malvasia, two grapes of average dullness. Many Italian whites are made from Trebbiano or blended with it, and it often makes a light, fairly neutral, average white plonk, albeit with good levels of crisp acidity. Malvasia is marginally more interesting, and usually produces wines with a deeper yellow-gold colour, more fatness and character. But not enough to make Frascati more than an average glugger.

2. *Orvieto*

A white wine from Umbria that comes either dry or off-dry. Sadly, at least 50% Trebbiano, which tells you all you need to know, really: not terribly exciting.

3. *Verdicchio*

An Italian white with character! Verdicchio is cultivated in two separate areas within the Marche region (halfway down the back edge of the 'boot'). The most widely planted regions are Castelli di Jesi DOC, not far from the coast, and the smaller Matelica DOC, further inland and higher up the hillsides. Good Verdicchio wines tend to have a deliciously concentrated, lemony flavour and an almondy finish. You often see them in amphora-shaped bottles. These wines can be interesting and complex, with a pleasing level of flavour.

4. *Montepulciano d'Abruzzo*

Montepulciano is a solid, workhorse grape grown in central Italy's Abruzzi region. Solid, dependable, if rough around the edges, Montepulciano can be a good-value, everyday glugger: a dark wine with big tannins and low acidity.

AND FINALLY: A FEW UP-AND-COMING
grape varieties

1. Fiano and Aglianico

You might come across these varieties from the Campania region in southern Italy, and both are worth a try. **FIANO** is a white grape that's getting more and more fashionable, although it remains relatively unknown in the wider world. It has a floral, peachy aroma and makes what can be described as a reasonably intensely flavoured Italian white. Quality and value are somewhat variable, but it is usually cheap enough to take a punt on if you see one. **AGLIANICO** also has a lot of potential; it's a dark-skinned red grape with big flavours and full body that's getting more and more attention. It yields powerful wines, but with ample supple tannins and enough acidity to hold it all in check. The two DOs that make the best are Taurasi and Aglianico del Vulture.

2. Negroamaro and Primitivo

Puglia is the 'heel' of Italy and it is bloody hot. As such, big, chunky, hearty high-alcohol reds are the order of the day. **NEGROAMARO** means 'dark bitter' in Italian, which hints at what this variety is: thick, dark and powerful. It might be a bit much to expect something subtle or nuanced from this part of the world, but some really good bottles out there are similar to a big New World red, but fashioned in a savoury, Old World style. Same goes for **PRIMITIVO**, which is genetically identical to the quintessential inky, liquorice-flavoured California Zinfandel (see California, page 165). Here it makes chunky, characterful wines with big structure and a herbal edge that's less frequently found in California.

3. Nero d'Avola

Sicily used to be known as an area specializing in cheap bulk wines. It's *scorchio*, and many wineries lacked modern equipment and hygiene levels. However, it has improved of late, with wineries such as Planeta, Duca di Salaparuta and Donnafugata producing fantastic wines. The local **NERO D'AVOLA** grape is particularly suited to this hot climate and makes some medium- to full-bodied, brooding, slightly herbal reds. Most Nero d'Avola you'll encounter is reasonably simple glugging stuff, but the best has good aging potential.

13

GERMANY

W henever I go into an independent wine shop, the German wines section is one of the first places I stop. Chances are this is where the bargains will be. Germany is still unfashionable, thanks to its 1960s, '70s and '80s bad patch of Blue Nun and Black Tower. You'd be amazed at how much these brands still sell, though – especially Black Tower, which remains phenomenally successful.

But, as Germany continues to produce Liebfraumilch by the shed-load, it also continues to make lots of extraordinarily good wines of real purity and beauty. Sadly, they're still overshadowed by the dross, but this only makes the good stuff cheaper for those in the know who understand that Germany doesn't just make rubbish. In fact, it also makes some of the most stunning white wines you're ever likely to come across.

Germany's big problem isn't just the lakes of plonk putting the diamond bottles in the shade. Other factors put it on the back foot. Pretty much every other factor you can think of, unfortunately, including:

COMMON VARIETIES

RED
Spätburgunder (Pinot Noir), Dornfelder

WHITE
Riesling, Müller-Thurgau, Sylvaner and Scheurebe

- Those thin, tapered, foot-long bottles that don't fit on the shelf and slide out of the rack.

- Tongue-twisting wine names. Rüdesheimer Rosengarten Schloss Whatsit Goldcapsule Grosses Gewächs doesn't exactly roll of the tongue.

- Gothic script and weird knotwork all over the labels – SO 1650s.

- Is it sweet? Is it dry? How sweet exactly? Why doesn't it JUST SAY??

Two of the four above are just packaging and presentation. OK, so the bottles and labels sometimes leave a bit to be desired, but if we knew the wine inside was amazing, we could get over that. The German language doesn't seem to lend itself to romantic wine descriptions; there are no simple names like 'Sancerre' or 'Burgundy' to work with. Surprisingly, though, German wine names are actually descriptive, accurate and no-nonsense (if you read German, that is). They tend to be a much more precise description of what you'll find in the bottle than French labels. For non-German-speakers, though, they can look too hard to remember, faintly medical and as if they contain too many 'g's. In reality, the problem lies with us. We just need to get used to them, grasp what they're rambling on about and learn a few key words. Start with these:

- **TROCKEN** Means dry.
- **HALBTROCKEN (LITERALLY 'HALF-DRY')** Means medium dry, i.e. dry enough to go with most savoury foods.

The level of sweetness/dryness is the most important issue when it comes to buying German wines. The reality is that the German approach to making wine is very different from that of the rest of the world. It's brilliant that they have such a distinctive ethos when it comes to winemaking as it adds to the richness of the wine world, but it does take a little understanding if you're not to pick up something unexpected. Stick with trocken wines and you won't buy any sweet ones accidentally.

Like the other main Old World countries, Germany has its various quality levels, and these are also changing due to new EU regulations:

1 **TAFELWEIN** (or just *Wein*) – Table wine. Probably *scheiße* (and you can look that one up yourself).

2 **LANDWEIN** (changing to *geschützte geographische Angabe*, or ggA) – Country wine. There are some good wines at this level, but unless you know what you're buying, it's no guarantee of quality.

3 **QUALITÄTSWEIN BESTIMMTER ANBAUGEBIETE** (QbA) – There are some very good and some less interesting wines at this level. Up to and including QbA level, wines can have sugar added before fermentation begins.

4 **QUALITÄTSWEIN MIT PRÄDIKAT** (QmP, changing to *geschützte Ursprungsbezeichnung, or gU*) – The top level of German wines, and by far the most interesting. Grapes that go into QmP/gU wines are fully ripe, so no sugar has been added here.

So, as a first rule of thumb: if the quality level stated on a bottle of German wine has three letters and starts with a Q, you're on safe ground.

THE GERMAN
sweetness/dryness issue

The highest level of German wines is QmP/gU, and, at this level, they're much more interesting. Producers aren't legally permitted to add sugar to these wines during vinification; they rely on natural grape sugar.

Germany is on the brink of being too far north to grow grapes to any acceptable level of ripeness; it's simply too cold. Therefore, German winemakers have to use a range of grape varieties, which we'll examine shortly, that cope well with cold weather. Because of this, these are rarely the same grapes you'll find in the New World or hotter Old World countries. In a good vintage, though, these grapes do ripen well, and this ripeness expresses itself in high natural grape-sugar levels.

These sweetness levels all have different names, and this designation is on the label somewhere. Ranging from dry to sweet, these are:

KABINETT
Dry (if it says *trocken* on the label) to medium-dry. Has nothing to do with 'Cabernet', just sounds a bit similar. Will age five to ten years.

SPÄTLESE
Medium to medium-sweet (or dry if it says *trocken* on the label.) Will age eight to 15 years.

AUSLESE
Sweet. Will age ten to 20 years, sometimes much longer.

TROCKENBEERENAUSLESE
(TBA) Very sweet, and affected by a desirable fungus called *Botrytis cinerea*, aka noble rot. Here, the *trocken* in the name refers to the state of the grapes when picked – i.e. 'raisined', with sugars concentrated by the friendly fungus – rather than the wine, which is very sweet. The best examples of TBA and Eiswein (left) can age up to 100 years.

EISWEIN
'Ice wine' made from grapes left to freeze on the vines (at around -8˚C), pressed to yield a small amount of intensely flavoured juice. Can be amazing – and it's amazingly expensive.

BEERENAUSLESE
(BA) Very sweet, usually affected by noble rot (see left).

No matter how sweet or dry, these wines should always be balanced with a beam of acidity shining through them; the higher the sugar content, the higher the level of acidity needed to ensure a wine isn't flabby or sickly sweet.

One notable advantage about German wines is that they tend to be low in alcohol: typically around 8-12% ABV.

This means they are often delicate in body and don't have a heavy feeling in the mouth, which lets the fruit flavours shine through. It also means you can drink twice as many delightful sips as you can with a bottle of California Chardonnay. Perfect lunchtime wines.

But when do you drink them? Kabinett and Spätlese *trocken* wines go well with a lot of dishes, particularly chicken, pork and fish, especially river fish and shellfish like crab. From here on up the sweetness scale, they're better paired with sweet dishes, fruit and cheeses. But they don't need to be paired with food; these wines are beautiful by themselves.

Often people think sweet wine should go at the end of a meal, but I'm coming around to the idea that it's better to have a small glass before a meal. Not only does it feel enticingly decadent to start on the sweet wine straight away, but sometimes it can be a bit too much at the end of a long meal, where spirits are a better bet, thanks to their digestive properties.

The other detail that can be stated on the label of a bottle of QmP/gU is the name of the *Einzellage*, or individual vineyard.

Vineyard sites are as important in Germany as anywhere else; the differences in quality and microclimate between two Einzellagen *can be huge. As in Burgundy, the name of the producer is also paramount.*

GERMAN VINTAGES
The 1999 vintage wasn't very good, but 2000 was a nightmare – avoid German 2000s; 2001, 2004 and 2005, however, were broadly very good, as well as 2007 and particularly 2009.

GERMAN
grape varieties

There really aren't that many German grapes that you need to know about, but here are the main contenders.

Riesling

Riesling is the most important in quality terms by a country mile. Germany's greatest wines are made from Riesling – you can't argue with that. Different areas all give different character to their Rieslings, because this is one grape that is very expressive of terroir.

There are a number or reasons why Riesling has, over the centuries, become the grape variety of choice.

1 It likes a long, slow ripening period: a real advantage so far north.

2 It grows well on a number of soils – limestone, granite, slate – all of which are found in Germany.

3 It holds its quality, even in larger yields.

4 It buds late, so avoids bud-killing spring frosts.

5 It is generally frost-resistant.

6 It is prone to botrytis/noble rot.

7 It is versatile, producing dry, sweet and sparkling styles.

8 It is a stunning variety and is capable of making some of the finest whites imaginable.

Silvaner

Silvaner (spelled with an 'i' instead of a 'y' in German) can also make some good wines, but it is rarely as interesting, complex or subtle as Riesling. It can produce some good less expensive sweet wines, though.

Müller-Thurgau

Müller-Thurgau, until recently, was the most widely planted grape variety in Germany. It would be easier if it were called 'Riesling-Madeleine Royal' because it is a crossing of these two varieties. But no, that would be too simple and easy to understand, wouldn't it, Germany?

Müller-Thurgau is an easy grape to grow, and it ripens early, which is handy in such a cool climate. On the other hand, it can all too easily produce flabby, boring wine that lacks character and appeal.

The long and short of it is, almost all wines from Müller-Thurgau aren't that exciting.

Liebfraumilch, Niersteiner, Piesporter Michelsberg (not to be confused with other potentially excellent Piesport appellations): these are some of the best-known and most-exported German wines, and you'll see them on the shelves of all European supermarkets. They're made from Müller-Thurgau, so don't bother. Stick to the regal Riesling.

Spätburgunder

Germany does make a little red wine, but you rarely see it outside the country because they drink it all. The principal grape used is Pinot Noir, here known as Spätburgunder. Red grapes take longer to ripen than white ones, and most German regions have a hard enough time ripening white ones as it is.

You might think there aren't many sites that can successfully ripen this variety in Germany, but in the right hands, Spätburgunder can be exquisite. It is pale, subtle, ethereal stuff, but can be highly complex and exhibit some fascinating aromas. If you see it, try it, but stick to the hotter vintages of 2003, 2005 and 2009 and the more southerly climes of Pfalz (see page 139) and Baden.

MOSEL

Most of Germany's wine-producing regions are in the south, as you'd expect in such a cool climate, and most are situated along riverbanks (so they can get exposure to optimum amounts of sunshine).

The Mosel is probably the best-known German region for producing fine white wines.

Riesling loves slate, and on the slate riverbanks of the Mosel, it creates some of its greatest expressions. It needs south-facing vineyards to ripen enough, but, thanks to its random snaking route, the river provides various workable sites. The Saar and the Ruwer are small tributaries of the Mosel, and both provide subtle variations on typical Mosel Riesling; the Saar gives austere wines with high acidity, whereas the Ruwer yields more subtle, floral expressions of the grape.

The Mosel grape-growing region itself starts at Koblenz, with some of the most celebrated vineyards in Germany producing typically highly grape-scented wines but with amazing clarity and brightness. Travel further down the valley, and eventually you'll reach Piesport. As mentioned before, Piesporter Michelsberg is rubbish, but that is far removed from fine Piesporter Riesling, which can be delicious.

SOME GOOD MOSEL PRODUCERS
J J Prüm, Egon Müller, Fritz Haag, Dr Loosen, von Kesselstatt, Maximin Grünhaus and Karthäuserhof

BE SURE TO TRY
Mosel Rieslings – low alcohol so perfect at lunchtime

MOSEL
Germany

RHEINGAU

RHEINGAU AGE-ABILITY
Compared to the wines of the Nahe, Pfalz and Rheinhessen, Rheingau wines are the longest-lived.

The Rheingau is a 40km/25-mile region that stretches along the river Rhein/Rhine, around 50km/31 miles east of the Mosel River. The wines of the Rheingau can have a power, fruitiness and spice not found in the subtle, crystalline wines of the Mosel, so, if you're looking for a Riesling with more *cojones*, the Rheingau might be more up your street.

Although there is some slate in the geology here, there's also a mix of other soils, which gives the Rieslings of the Rheingau their fullness and power.

The Rheingau's climate is typically warmer and sunnier than that of the Mosel – so much so that even some red wine is made here.

SOME GOOD RHEINGAU PRODUCERS
The eastern part is home to the two great *schlösse*, or castles: Schloss Johannisberg and Schloss Vollrads, both of which make outstanding wines. Other producers worth searching out are Leitz and Johannishof.

PFALZ

The Pfalz is a fat stretch of land located due south of the Rheingau and is the driest region in Germany.

The Mosel and the Rheingau are all about Riesling and its multifarious expressions, but the Pfalz is different: it doesn't only make Riesling, but concentrates instead on other grape varieties.

The Pfalz makes some excellent Spätburgunders and even some good Sauvignon Blanc. As such, the winemakers here use more varied production methods, such as aging in oak (Riesling doesn't take to maturing in wood). The further south you go, however, the more Riesling starts cropping up, albeit a more powerful style on the whole compared to its northern neighbours.

SOME GOOD PFALZ PRODUCERS
These can be extraordinarily good, and very decent value. Look for Dr Bürklin-Wolf, Reichsrat von Buhl and Lingenfelder.

HUGE VARIETY
There are 45 white grape varieties grown in the Pfalz

PFALZ
Germany

14

PORTUGAL

The most famous wine of Portugal is undoubtedly Port: a fortified sweet red that is covered on page 176. Port is such a fascinating, varied and venerable wine that it might make sense to assume the normal red and white wines of Portugal have always been equally interesting. Historically, though, Portuguese reds have been harsh, over-alcoholic and pretty rough around the edges, the whites a bit flabby and oxidized. Fortunately, this situation has changed, and some wonderful reds and increasingly good whites are being produced. There are several reasons why the reds and whites of Portugal have great potential:

red that is covered on page 176.

- Many areas have favourable climates: hot, dry and with plenty of sun.

- Much of the soil is poor and well-drained.

- Most importantly, the country has a huge variety of well-endowed indigenous grapes capable of making excellent wines.

COMMON VARIETIES

RED
Touriga Nacional, Tinta Roriz (Tempranillo) and Alfrocheiro

WHITE
Arinto, Alvarinho, Encruzado and Malvasia

The two main regions for reds lie in the north: Dão and the Douro. The Douro is more famous for Port, but many of the grapes used in Port production adapt to red-wine production, especially Tinta Roriz (aka Tempranillo) and Touriga Nacional. Varietal Touriga Nacional in particular is well worth trying; the best has a good concentration of fruit but with fresh acidity and a wonderful floral element reminiscent of roses. Dão wines used to be awful, but they have reinvented themselves over the last 15 years or so. More Touriga Nacional here, but also spicy Alfrocheiro and lighter, fruitier Jaen; the full-bodied whites from the Encruzado grape are also worth a look.

Southern Portugal tends to make burlier, powerful reds. The three main regions are Alentejo, Ribatejo and Estremadura. If you're a fan of New World reds, you should dip your toe in here, as quality is increasing, with many good-value wines made very much in the New World style. The grapes are Aragonês (Tempranillo) and Trincadeira, but you'll also find the ubiquitous Cabernet Sauvignon and Syrah.

One white the Portuguese been doing well for centuries, though, is Vinho Verde. Literally 'green wine', the name refers to the fact that it should be drunk young. It's made from a blend of local grapes, but the best often comes from Alvarinho (Spanish Albariño). It's a pale white wine with high acidity, low alcohol and a slight sparkle. Can be a bit plain, but it's frequently a good-value, refreshing white.

SOME GOOD PORTUGUESE PRODUCERS
Quinta do Crasto, Wine and Soul, Quinta de l'Infantado, Quinta de Chocapalha, Niepoort, Quinta de la Rosa

15

REST of EUROPE

H istorically, France, Italy, Spain, Germany and Portugal have been the most important European countries in terms of winemaking, but most Old World countries have some history of winemaking. However, wines produced in the likes of Georgia, Morocco, Luxembourg, Holland, Slovenia, Belgium or Macedonia are virtually never seen outside their homelands. Either too little is made to export, or it's so excruciatingly bad that no one would drink it if it were. You can find the odd bottle from the following countries, though – and some of it is brilliant.

AUSTRIA

It's not easy to track down Austrian wine, but when you do, get excited. It's similar to that produced in Germany and Alsace, with lots of Riesling, Blauburgunder (aka Pinot Noir), and Blaufränkisch, a good-quality red grape that typically creates medium-bodied, sappy reds with high acidity.

Austria uses pretty much the same label categories as Germany when it comes to stating sweetness levels. The national speciality, however, is Grüner Veltliner. It's a name that hardly trips off the tongue (*GROON-er velt-LEEN-er*) but it's worth remembering as it is one of the most exciting white grape varieties around and can result in delicious white wines.

Grüner Veltliner belongs in the camp that includes Pinot Gris, Torrontés and Albariño – medium-bodied, undervalued tangy whites with loads of flavour. It usually has a spicy, grapefruity flavour with a distinctive white-pepper finish.

As far as reds are concerned, as well as Blauburgunder and Blaufränkisch, Austrians grow a lot of Zweigelt. Not only can this make good, full-bodied reds with nice bite and acidity, it can also be very handy to know about when playing Scrabble.

COMMON VARIETIES

RED
Blauburgunder,
Blaufränkisch, Zweigelt

WHITE
Grüner Veltliner, Riesling,

SOME GOOD AUSTRIAN PRODUCERS
Fred Loimer, Nikolaihof,
Franz Prager, Willi Opitz,
Kurt Angerer,
Weingut Pittnauer

143

GREECE

Although the Greeks have been fermenting grapes for 4,000 years, it's only in the last 25 that their wines have been decent enough to bottle and sell in other countries. According to Homer, wine was used in all areas of life in ancient times: as food, as medicine, during festivals, and also in a spiritual context. Pretty advanced, those ancient Greeks. Greeks today have around 300 indigenous grape varieties, and almost all of the country's production comes from them. Only a few are worth mentioning here, though, partly because they have names that sound like characters out of a Greek *X-Men* movie.

1 **XYNOMAVRO** Literally 'acid black'. Can be harsh and acidic when young, but softens as it ages. Good, but go for older vintages. Look for Naoussa, which is aged in oak barrels.

2 **MAVRODAPHNE** A powerful, dark-skinned variety normally used to make a Port-like sweet wine.

3 **ASSYRTIKO** Top-quality white, often from the island of Santorini. Dry, with good levels of refreshing acidity. Well worth a try.

And how could we forget Retsina? This isn't a type of grape, however; it's a style of wine, normally made from the Savatiano grape. Pine resin is added to the wine during fermentation, which gives it an aromatic, pine flavour. It's never that amazing, but can sometimes be enjoyable with local food – just don't bring any back: it won't be the same.

SOME GOOD GREEK PRODUCERS
Greek wines tend to be quite pricey but have a lovely individual style. Try Hatzidakis, Alpha, Ktima Biblia Chora, Gaia and Nassiakos.

HUNGARY

Hungary makes some good wines, particularly medium- to full-bodied reds such as Egri Bikavér (aka Bulls' Blood) and other wines from the Kékfrankos grape (the local name for Blaufränkisch).

The one Hungarian wine you really need to know about, however, is Tokáji (TOK-eye), a golden sweet wine.

For years it was considered one of the greatest wines in the world, but under communist rule, quality plummeted. They've since sorted it out, and a good Tokáji is a beautiful wine. The grapes are affected by noble rot (see page 133), and the wine should have the typical mushroom/marmalade flavours often associated with nobly rotten grapes. It spends at least a couple of years in wooden barrels, where some of it matures underneath a film of bacteria, not unlike the 'flor' that grows on certain Sherries. It also has notably high acidity that cuts through its syrupiness like a knife. The sweetness level is measured in *puttonyos* (a *puttony* was originally the weight of a hod of grapes); five or six *puttonyos* is a good sign. Can be useful for matching with desserts, particularly sweet ones with high acidity.

SOME GOOD TOKÁJI PRODUCERS

Royal Tokáji wines are reliably high quality, and Dobogó, Oremus and István Szepsy make brilliant examples, too.

ROMANIA

Romania actually produces quite a lot of wine but doesn't export much of it. That's OK, though. The majority are plain, flabby whites made from local varieties. They do make some good-quality, fairly full-bodied reds from the likes of Cabernet Sauvignon and Merlot and local varieties such as Fetească Neagră, Novac and Negru de Dragănşāni.

Some good aromatic whites come from Transylvania; some decent Chardonnay from Murfatlar. But, on the whole, we're in the 'I'm looking for something cheap to make mulled wine with' territory here...

COMMON VARIETIES

WHITE
Chardonnay, Pinot Gris, Sauvignon Blanc

RED
Cabernet Sauvignon, Merlot, Fetească Neagră, Novac, Negru de Dragănşāni

BULGARIA

Bulgaria has a long, distinguished history of winemaking with a long list of decent (and not so decent) grape varieties. Most wines these days are made from international varieties, though – which is sad, since there are so many excellent examples of Cabernet Sauvignon, Chardonnay or Merlot from around the world to contend with. Still, these wines can be reasonably good value and they're often very cheap. Most wine-drinkers don't seem willing to spend more than a few pounds on a bottle of Bulgarian wine – a shame when investment is needed to help the industry grow and quality improve. Undoubtedly there are bargains to be had, but it's hard to get that excited about Bulgarian wines right now.

SLOVENIA

Since the break-up of the former Yugoslavia, Slovenia has been the most successful republic in developing a wine industry. Most of what it makes is light, crisp and aromatic white, mainly single varieties: Riesling, Chardonnay, Pinot Gris, Pinot Blanc and Sauvignon Blanc. The bulk of what's produced, however, comes from local varieties Laški Rizling (aka Welschriesling, a light-bodied, plain white grape; no relation to Riesling) and Šipon (the Furmint of Hungary). You also see a bit of red, usually from lighter grapes such as Pinot Noir, Zweigelt or Blaufränkisch, and some fuller reds from Cabernet Sauvignon and Merlot. Almost all Slovenian wine is drunk locally, but more is being sneaked out for the rest of us to enjoy.

SWITZERLAND

The Swiss make some very good wine, both red and white, but it's either expensive or often yawn-worthy at the affordable end. The main white grape is Chasselas, which is about as exciting as Ugni Blanc (i.e. not very). In red, it's often Pinot Noir, which rarely gets the pulse racing here like it does in France, New Zealand, Oregon or Germany.

UNITED KINGDOM

I'd love to be able to proclaim that British wines are every bit as good as the best from the rest of the world, but if I did, you probably wouldn't believe me. Sad to say, my pants would indeed catch fire, but at least it's true to say that they're getting better all the time.

Most British vineyards are in southeast England, around Sussex and Kent, but there are a number in Cornwall and south Wales, and even as far north as Yorkshire. Growing grapes in the UK is always tricky; there are so many potential problems, from disease and frost to rot or just not enough sun. Most of the grapes we use over here are German varieties, since we also have to contend with a very cool, marginal climate for grape-growing.

Chardonnay and Pinot Noir are being planted, mainly for sparkling-wine production – the one area in which we do excel. Southern England shares the same chalk on which Champagne grows its vines, and the climate isn't that far off Champagne's in certain areas. Some (but not all) British sparkling wines are world-class. They're rarely cheap; most vineyards are pretty small and fairly recently established, and winemakers here have to work in challenging conditions, but do give them a try. You can even do that at the wineries themselves, since many have visitor centres and restaurants. For a list of ones to visit, see the appendix on page 184.

SOME GOOD BRITISH PRODUCERS
The whites and sparkling wines are still the best (try Gusbourne, Ridgeview or Nyetimber). But one red in particular deserves a mention, and that's Bolney Wine Estate's Foxhole Vineyard Pinot Noir.

LEBANON

You might think I'm just trying to be clever by putting Lebanon in here, but against all expectations, Lebanese producers actually make a fair few good wines, and they do tend to be more Old World in style. The best is Chateau Musar, the original great wine from Lebanon. There's a fair bit of variation between vintages (and bottles) of Musar, but on the whole they make flavoursome, opulent Bordeaux-like wines from Cabernet Sauvignon, Cinsault and Carignan. Widely available and well worth a try.

SOME GOOD LEBANESE PRODUCERS
Also try wines from Chateau Kefraya and Chateau Ksara – pretty good, too.

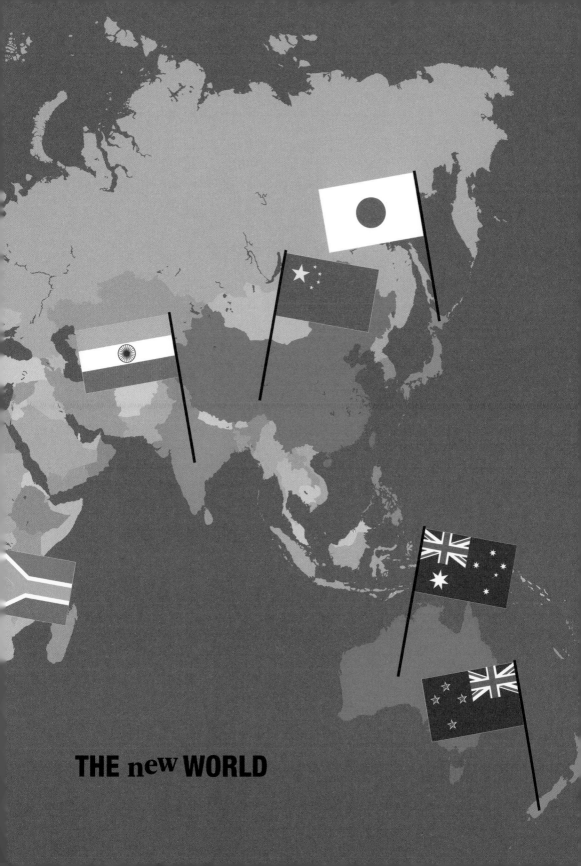

THE new WORLD

16

AUSTRALIA

A ustralia is a hulking great land mass, but it's only the sixth-largest wine-producing nation by volume (behind Argentina). Only a small part of Oz makes wine; the rest is just too hot and dry. Wine-producing areas are centred around either end of the southern coast. There's a bit in the southwest, around Perth in Western Australia, but most is in the southeast, in South Australia, New South Wales and Victoria.

One misconception about Australian wine is that it's cheap. In reality, you'll pay at least the same as for French wine if you want an interesting bottle.

Wines produced on the scale of the Hardys Stamp of Australia range can be decent but rarely exciting. They're made in vast industrial wineries by big companies whose primary aim is maximizing profit. Obviously, some branded wines are better than others. Of those listed below, the ones with * I like, the ones with ** I love.

COMMON VARIETIES

RED
Shiraz (Syrah), Cabernet Sauvignon, Merlot, Pinot Noir, Grenache, Mourvèdre

WHITE
Chardonnay, Sauvignon Blanc, Semillon, Riesling

** Peter Lehmann	* Brown Brothers	Lindemans
** Yalumba	* Penfolds	Hardys
(which owns	* Wolf Blass	Rosemount
* Oxford Landing)	* Jacob's Creek	Yellow Tail

A brand's range can have dozens of different wines, from red to white, dry, sweet and everyday to premium. There are bound to be some good ones and some duff ones among them, so it's hard to generalize. Penfolds' Grange, for example, is often cited as one of the best wines in the New World, and some Wolf Blass premium wines are superb, as are some of Hardys'. The cheapest in these ranges are fine, if not exciting.

Big brands can be useful in terms of remembering a decent wine, and they also offer an easy way of trying unfamiliar grape varieties. If a brand make a decent Cabernet Sauvignon, chances are its Semillon (spelled here without an é) won't be too bad. Needless to say, though, thousands of brilliant Australian wines are made by smaller producers: much better than the majority of the supermarket stuff.

There are two good ways to explore Australia (and New World wines in general) without getting caught up in big brands. The first is to explore the country region by region. Regionality is becoming increasingly important in the best Aussie wines, and it's worth knowing a few areas and their specialities to get the most out of them. The second way is to pick a grape, such as Shiraz, and try bottles from different regions to see how each interprets the variety. And, if you like one wine in particular, you can see what else is made by the same winery and explore that, too.

151

Barossa (South Australia)

ALSO TRY Grenache, Mourvèdre

GOOD PRODUCERS Glaetzer, Torbreck, Turkey Flat, John Duval, St Hallett

North of Adelaide, probably the best-known winemaking area in Oz. Large plantings of old vines, up to 150 years, which produce some excellent fruit.

McLaren Vale (South Australia)

ALSO TRY Grenache, Cabernet Sauvignon

GOOD PRODUCERS Kay Brothers, Pertaringa, Mitolo, d'Arenberg, Wirra Wirra

South of Adelaide, with a cooler climate, thanks to the ocean influence. McLaren Vale still makes powerful wines; big, bold reds and pungent, fruity whites.

Clare Valley (South Australia)

ALSO TRY Shiraz, Cabernet Sauvignon

GOOD PRODUCERS Grosset, Mount Horrocks, Knappstein, Jim Barry, Kilikanoon

Source of some of Oz's best Riesling. Typically dry, fragrant, with high acidity.

Hunter Valley (New South Wales)

ALSO TRY Chardonnay, Shiraz

GOOD PRODUCERS Brokenwood, Tyrell's, Clonakilla

Some 129km (80 miles) north of Sydney, the best place for Semillon in Australia, probably the world. Semillon has a limey aroma. It makes sweet and dry styles, but Hunter wines are dry, often with low alcohol. Semillon from this area is best between ten and 20 years old. At this stage, it can get honeyed and nutty. Chardonnays can be good, too: soft, round and peachy. Hunter Shiraz can be very long-lived, and is distinctive: earthy, meaty, leathery, the style best described by the tasting note 'sweaty saddle'. As in a horse's saddle you've been riding in all day. In the sun. Nice.

Coonawarra (South Australia)

ALSO TRY Chardonnay, Shiraz

GOOD PRODUCERS Petaluma, Hollick, Parker

Relatively cool; makes some of the best Cabernet Sauvignon in Oz, often with a distinctive eucalyptus aroma. Many of the best grow on terra rossa (red earth).

Margaret River (Western Australia)

ALSO TRY Riesling, Pinot Noir

GOOD PRODUCERS Cape Mentelle, Cullen, Leeuwin Estate, Moss Wood

Margaret River is at the southwestern tip of Australia. It's relatively cool and wet, so its wines are different from those of South Australia and Victoria: lighter in body and alcohol, more delicate and graceful, more aromatic.

BEST FOR Shiraz, Cabernet Sauvignon, Sauvignon Blanc, Chardonnay, Semillon

Yarra Valley (Victoria)

ALSO TRY Chardonnay, Cabernet Sauvignon

GOOD PRODUCERS Mac Forbes, Giant Steps, Yarra Yering

Has a cooler climate perfect for Pinot Noir and more elegant Chardonnay. Widely considered the best region for Pinot Noir in Oz. Decent sparkling, too.

BEST FOR Pinot Noir

Eden Valley (South Australia)

ALSO TRY Shiraz

GOOD PRODUCERS Henschke, Pewsey Vale

Very good, particularly long-lived Riesling, and some top Shiraz.

BEST FOR Riesling

Tasmania

ALSO TRY Riesling, Sauvignon Blanc

GOOD PRODUCERS Pirie, Tamar Ridge, Domaine A/Stony Vineyard

Fascinating island off the coast of South Australia, making some brilliant wines. Mostly cooler-climate varieties such as Chardonnay and Pinot Noir, both in still and sparkling form. Bags of potential, and diverse styles.

BEST FOR Chardonnay, Pinot Noir, sparkling wines

Rutherglen (Victoria)

GOOD PRODUCERS Stanton & Killeen, Campbells

Liqueur Muscat is a style unique to Australia. If you've never tried it, give it a whirl. It's a thick, amber, super-sweet, unctuous, decadent syrup of a wine, similar to Madeira or tawny Port (see pages 181 and 178). The grapes shrivel on the vine, then are slowly fermented and fortified with grape spirit. The wine is put into barrels and left in very hot sheds, where it takes on a toffee/caramel flavour. Topaque is similar but a little lighter in colour. They don't improve in bottle – but they don't need to.

BEST FOR Liqueur Muscat, Topaque

17

NEW ZEALAND

Because we think of it as being so geographically close to Australia, it's all too easy to lump New Zealand and Australia together when thinking about wine, but the two countries are completely different. Australia has been making wine for over 200 years, is pretty broad in what it produces and has a number of distinct regions. It churns out a massive amount of wine, a lot of which is everyday, branded glugging stuff. New Zealand, on the other hand, doesn't have the wide range Australia has, but what it does, it tends to do very well.

New Zealand has been making wine in commercial quantities only since the 1970s. It has always been a conservative country when it comes to alcohol; restaurants were first allowed to sell wine in 1960; supermarkets in 1990 (and beer in supermarkets only since 1999!). Although a late starter, its progress has been staggering, but it still produces just about a tenth of what Australia does.

This country has the most southerly vineyards in the world, and a cooler, wetter climate than Australia's. When thinking about New Zealand, think more along the lines of Germany and northern France (Loire, Burgundy, Alsace). Like them, New Zealand's climate borders on the outer limits of wine production, and because of this, it grows similar grape varieties: Sauvignon Blanc, Gewürztraminer, Riesling, Pinot Gris, Chardonnay and Pinot Noir. A fair bit of Cabernet Sauvignon, Merlot, Syrah and various others are also grown here, but on a lesser scale due to the cool climate.

Although New Zealand doesn't provide unique grape varieties or styles, it does make a lot of reliable, high-quality wines: ripe, fresh and aromatic, with delicious fruit flavours. As its winemaking industry develops and more grape varieties are matched to specific sites, these wines are only going to get more and more exciting.

COMMON VARIETIES

RED
Cabernet Sauvignon, Merlot, Syrah, Pinot Noir

WHITE
Sauvignon Blanc, Chardonnay, Pinot Gris, Gewürztraminer, Riesling

Although famous (rightly so) for its Sauvignon Blanc, New Zealand is much more than a one-trick pony.

Of course, Sauvignon Blanc can make excellent wine, but it rarely ever produces anything that completely blows you away. Riesling, Chardonnay, Pinot Noir, and Cabernet Sauvignon, on the other hand – now they're capable of making the greatest wines in the world.

New Zealand has a fair few large brands of its own that are seen in the UK, but most are reasonably reliable. Of those listed below, the ones with * I like, the ones with ** I love.

** Tinpot Hut	* Villa Maria	Montana
** Mud House	* Southbank Estate	(now known
** Isabel Estate	* Wither Hills	as Brancott Estate)
	* Saint Clair Family Estate	Oyster Bay

Almost all of the wines bearing these brands on their labels are at least decent, well-made and drinkable. Some that are produced by the better companies are extremely good; some of the Montana and Oyster Bay reds could do with some work.

As New Zealand's winemakers experiment with grape varieties and regions, regionality is becoming more and more important. Below are the main winemaking regions that are worth exploring:

BEST FOR
Sauvignon Blanc

Marlborough (South Island)

ALSO TRY Chardonnay, Pinot Noir
GOOD PRODUCERS Yealands, Dog Point, Clos Henri, Framingham, Greywacke, Delta, Cloudy Bay

Marlborough is New Zealand's largest wine-producing region, on the northern tip of South Island. New Zealand first came to the fore with Marlborough Sauvignon Blanc, and it's now recognized as one of the world's classic wine styles. It's more fruity than the Loire/Sancerre style of Sauvignon Blanc as a rule, but it doesn't get as tropical as Chilean examples; it retains those pungent, aromatic, grassy gooseberry flavours that make Sauvignon Blanc so unique and delicious.

If you haven't heard of Cloudy Bay, it was the first New Zealand Sauvignon Blanc to grab the world's attention, and it became a cult wine almost overnight. These days, lots of similar-quality wines are available at lower prices, but the Cloudy Bay brand remains strong and commands big bucks. Other whites from Marlborough are worth trying, too, particularly its fresh Chardonnays and Rieslings.

MARLBOROUGH
New Zealand

THE 'MARLBOROUGH GRAPE'
While over half of all wine made in New Zealand is Sauvignon Blanc, the bulk of this comes from a single region – Marlborough.

Hawke's Bay (North Island)

ALSO TRY Chardonnay
GOOD PRODUCERS Thornbury, Craggy Range, Bilancia, Trinity Hill

BEST FOR
Syrah, Cabernet
Sauvignon,
Merlot

Hawke's Bay is another great region for wine in New Zealand. It's a fair bit warmer and sunnier than Marlborough, and so it's more suited to red wines and Chardonnay than Sauvignon Blanc. Its Chardonnays tend to be citric and fresh but full. Look for wines from the Gimblett Gravels designated area: an excellent area for fuller-bodied New Zealand reds.

Central Otago (South Island)

ALSO TRY Chardonnay, Pinot Gris, Riesling
GOOD PRODUCERS Felton Road, Mt Difficulty, Wild Earth Vineyards

BEST FOR
Pinot Noir

New Zealand Pinot Noir has been available over here only for the past ten years or so, which in the history of wine is barely a blink.

Central Otago, however, is increasingly becoming established as one of the best Pinot Noir-producing areas in the New World.

These are the most southerly vineyards of any country, far from the equator and therefore pretty cool; as such, you might not expect them to try ripening red grapes here. But, with the help of sloping hillside sites that give the fruit better exposure to sunshine, Pinot Noir can achieve ripeness and concentration. These wines don't yet attain the complexity of top Burgundy, but they can be delicious and well-balanced, with beautiful pure-fruit aromas. As the vines mature, the wines are likely to get better still.

18

SOUTH AFRICA

Wine isn't the first thing that springs to mind when you think of Africa. It makes a decent amount, but only at the northern- and southernmost tips; the vast swathe in between is just too hot and dry. They make a bit in Morocco (some drinkable), Tunisia and Algeria (less so) and they make a lot in South Africa, mostly around Cape Town. It has an almost Mediterranean climate there, although the sun does get hotter.

To call South Africa a 'New World' country is more of a statement about its wine styles than about how long wine has been made here.

The country's first recorded vintage goes back to 1652, so compared to New Zealand, it's pretty 'Old World', really. During the twentieth century, South Africa was best known for making Sherry- and Port-style wines, as well as base wines for distilling into brandy and grape spirit. The industry was very much geared towards quantity over quality, but better-quality estates have sprung up over the past 30 years.

Considering that it has been making wine for so long, though, South Africa hasn't brought too many new styles to the party. It tends to hammer out mostly varietal wines from the usual suspects: Chardonnay, Sauvignon Blanc, Semillon, Riesling, Cabernet Sauvignon, Merlot, Cabernet Franc, Shiraz, Pinot Noir and a handful of others. That's not to say that South African wines don't have their own take on things; they do. And it's becoming better and better.

Historically, there was one wine for which South Africa was justly famous: Constantia. This was a sweet wine made from Muscat de Frontignan (one of the many varieties of Muscat grown here) that was produced in the Constantia region just near Cape Town. In the late eighteenth-century Constantia was considered one of the greatest wines ever made. At least, that was the case until the vineyards were devastated by phylloxera (see page 12), and production ceased. Once winemakers had got to grips with this menace, a lot of replanting took place across all wine-producing regions, the majority consisting of just two varieties: Chenin Blanc and Pinotage.

Chenin Blanc is nothing if not versatile, producing dry, sweet, sparkling and dessert wines.

At its best, Chenin (or 'Steen' as they sometimes call it in South Africa) is capable of making exceptionally good wine. Sadly, most of the cheaper Chenin that comes from South Africa is bland, but some from top producers like Graham Beck, de Trafford and Ken Forrester are definitely worth checking out.

COMMON VARIETIES

RED
Pinotage, Cabernet Sauvignon, Cabernet Franc, Merlot, Shiraz

WHITE
Chardonnay, Sauvignon Blanc, Chenin Blanc

Pinotage's history begins with Cinsaut. This grape was widely planted to begin with, but it made a lot of fairly unremarkable wine, often due to winemakers encouraging huge crops of grapes that lacked concentrated flavours. Cinsaut is indigenous to the south of France (where it's more often spelled Cinsault), and usually found in blends in the Languedoc, Châteauneuf-du-Pape and Provence. Typically it's a medium-bodied, soft, fruity red with good acidity and often a floral aroma. When crossed with Pinot Noir, it created a new variety named Pinotage (the Cinsaut grape used to be called 'Hermitage' in South Africa, so it was a cross between the two names).

Pinotage can make good wine, but it's not everyone's cup of tea. Treated with care, and particularly when using fruit from older vines, Pinotage can make a full-bodied red, pretty high in tannin and acidity, with intense, dark-fruit flavours. If it says 'Cape Blend' on the label, there's Pinotage in it.

There aren't that many big South African brands, but of those listed below, the ones with * I like, the ones with ** I love:

** Jordan	* Fleur du Cap	KWV
** Vergelegen	* Beyerskloof	Kumala
** Meerlust	* Spier	Arniston Bay
		First Cape

Constantia

ALSO TRY Sauvignon Blanc

BEST FOR
Sweet Muscat

Constantia is a little peninsula jutting out into the sea south of Cape Town. It's a relatively cool, wet region, well suited to Sauvignon Blanc. Additionally, this is the home of a sweet wine known as 'Constantia' in Dickens's *Edwin Drood*. It's being produced again as 'Vin de Constance' by the Klein Constantia estate, which used original vineyard records for grape selection and guidance. Worth a look if you like sweet wines. It's wonderful stuff.

SOME GOOD CONSTANTIA PRODUCERS
Klein Constantia,
Groot Constantia,
Constantia Uitsig

CONSTANTIA
South Africa

Stellenbosch

ALSO TRY Chardonnay, Sauvignon Blanc

Sitting just above the northeast corner of
False Bay, Stellenbosch is South Africa's oldest
wine-producing region after Constantia, and
it's the heart of wine country, with the greatest number of famous estates.
It's also the place to look if you want to explore South African reds. This
area is situated near the coast, so the cool sea breezes make for more
subtle wines than some areas further inland.

Paarl

Just up the road, 24km (15 miles) north of Stellenbosch, is Paarl
(literally 'pearl'). It was once the heart of the Sherry- and Port-style
wine industry in South Africa, but today it's increasingly producing
good unfortified table wines.

Walker Bay

ALSO TRY Chardonnay, Sauvignon Blanc

An up-and-coming area, Walker Bay is cool, thanks both to its proximity
to the sea and to its vineyards being planted at high altitude. Not many
estates are producing wines here yet; however, those that are have had some
amazing results, particularly with Pinot Noir, which has been less successful
elsewhere in South Africa.

WALKER BAY
South Africa

19

NORTH AMERICA

W hen it comes to winemaking in the USA, the old West Coast/East Coast rivalry was settled long ago: California is the boss, and everybody knows it. A few other regions make a decent volume of good-quality wine (Oregon, Washington State, New York State, Virginia), but they are rarely found outside of the US, although some can be really excellent. Many states in the USA make wine, in fact, but often in such small quantities it doesn't get exported. California, however, is a different story.

CALIFORNIA

California is very much a land of extremes when it comes to wine. On the one hand, there are the neverending expanses of vineyards devoted to huge monoculture agribusiness: massive industrial-scale winemaking by the big names seen in all the supermarkets. On the other, there are hundreds of tiny boutique wineries run by wine nuts and hobbyists.

Although just one state among many, California makes a phenomenal amount of wine: 90% in fact, of all wine produced in the USA.

At one extreme, 'The Golden State' churns out titanic amounts of very cheap wine, often technically correct, if uninspiring and insipid. A lot of the sub-£6 stuff on the shelves in the UK is Californian, much of it from the hot, dry Central Valley. At the other extreme, to get your hands on a bottle from any of the top cult producers, you could be looking at over £1,000 (e.g. Screaming Eagle, Harlan Estate, Sine Qua Non). Even if you have the cash, getting hold of it isn't easy; try buying direct from a winery and it could take years to get on their mailing list – and, even then, you'll be limited to just a few bottles per person.

Are these wines really worth the money? At the top end, prices rival those of the very finest wines of France, with its centuries of winemaking heritage and experience. Yet just because the Old World has been making wine longer than the New World doesn't necessarily mean the New World can't produce wines of equal quality. This was brilliantly demonstrated in the so-called 'Judgement of Paris' tasting, organized in 1976 in Paris by Steven Spurrier (wine-shop owner turned respected wine journalist). The most important names in the French

COMMON VARIETIES

RED
Cabernet Sauvignon, Merlot, Syrah, Grenache, Zinfandel, Ruby Cabernet, Pinot Noir

WHITE
Chardonnay, Sauvignon Blanc (aka Fumé Blanc), Viognier, White Grenache

wine world were assembled to taste some of the best Cabernet Sauvignons (all from Bordeaux) and best Chardonnays (all from Burgundy) France had to offer. These were tasted alongside the best Cabernets and Chardonnays of California. All the wines were tasted 'blind', which means no one knew what they were tasting; the wines were poured from unmarked bottles into unmarked glasses.

When the marks were added up at the end, California wines came out on top – for both reds and whites. In your FACE, French wine snobs!

This did untold good for the image (and pricing) of New World wines – and undoubtedly a fair bit of damage to the accepted notion of French superiority.

Another reason California wine prices soar is when they get a good score from a certain American wine critic by the name of Robert Parker Jr. Few critics wield such power in their chosen field. Parker publishes a text-only newsletter each month called *The Wine Advocate*, in which he tastes wines and gives them a score out of 100. Getting a 100-point RP score is the holy grail for many winemakers, because it means they will become known the world over among wine enthusiasts, and the price for their wine will shoot through the roof. In all probability, this will give them a chance to increase the prices of all their wines in expectation of hugely increased demand.

Parker's influence is most keenly felt in the USA, but it has a global impact on wine prices. Like any wine-lover, Parker has personal likes and dislikes, and it's very difficult to be entirely objective all the time, whatever your field. Often wines that he marks high have similar characteristics: red wines with intense, ripe fruit flavours and a lot of oak, for instance. As winemakers across the world see the 'Parker effect' on wine prices, some of them adjust their wines towards this style in hopes of gaining higher Parker points. Which is great if you like drinking big, potent, ripe red wines all the time, but not so good if you don't. It's probably fair to say, though, that you don't often see these cult wines on the shelves in your local wine shop.

Most California wines, like so many New World wines, are varietal, made from Chardonnay and Cabernet Sauvignon in particular. Generally speaking, they tend to be high in alcohol and body with intense fruit flavours and an often liberal use of oak. The dry whites and reds sometimes have a touch more sweetness than those from other countries.

Californians aren't afraid to experiment, however, and often try out unusual grape varieties and blends in the hunt for something new – which is brilliant when it comes to keeping us interested and entertained as wine drinkers. Yet, as already mentioned, California wines are often quite expensive; if you're after good value, this is rarely the place to look, especially at the cheaper end.

Brands, again, are of vital importance in the California wine industry. Of those listed below, the ones with * I like, the one with ** I love.

** Ravenswood	Sutter Home
* Kendall Jackson	Blossom Hill
* Robert Mondavi	Echo Falls
* Fetzer	Ernest & Julio Gallo

For some reason, many of the big branded wines of California are particularly dull compared to those from most other countries. I tasted the entire Blossom Hill range a little while ago, and it was as stimulating as waiting in a queue to buy a train ticket. To be fair, they didn't taste disgusting – it's just that, compared to so many wines, what they're currently making isn't exciting at all.

One grape variety that California has made its own is **ZINFANDEL**. As mentioned previously, Zinfandel is none other than a clone of the Italian grape Primitivo, but it does make a distinctly different wine in California to what it makes in Italy. In California it yields intense red wines with concentrated red-and black-fruit flavours, typically with notes of liquorice and spice. They tend to be big, high-alcohol wines with high acidity and soft tannins.

At the top end they can be totally delicious, complex and intense, at the cheaper end you're talking quintessential barbecue wines. If you're a fan of Aussie Shiraz, try a bottle of California Zin. (N.B. the same does *not* go for the rosé known as White Zinfandel – this usually tastes faintly like a bag full of penny sweets that has spent too long in someone's pocket, as does California White Grenache).

Many other grape varieties also do well in California and are grown throughout the state. Some Viognier can be interesting, for example, but sometimes it's a little overblown. Some good Syrahs are coming through now, more often in the vein of Aussie Shiraz than French Syrah, and there have also been some reasonably successful experiments with Sangiovese.

All in all, California produces some staggering wines, but be prepared to pay for them.

Often, the style is big, powerful and alcoholic, but then many people love blockbuster wines; if you do, then California is a great place to explore. If subtlety, grace and understatement are your preferences, you'll have to look a bit harder. When firing on all cylinders, though, California wine can be truly awesome.

Of course, California is a huge state, with many differing regions, each imposing its own style on its wine. However, there seems less concentration here on specific terroirs than in Australia and New Zealand, and more emphasis on winemakers and winemaking practices. Although the number of smaller regions south of San Francisco are doing some great things (notably Santa Cruz), Napa and Sonoma are still the most important wine areas to get to know here.

Napa Valley
ALSO TRY Chardonnay

BEST FOR
Cabernet Sauvignon

Napa Valley is the most famous wine region in California, with good reason. Though it creates only 4% of California's wine output by volume, this equates to 20% by value. It's known foremost for its Cabernet Sauvignons and Chardonnays, both of which can be profoundly brilliant wines. Its Cabernets range from big, powerful wines with lovely berry fruit and a distinctive herbal edge to more restrained, understated European styles. Its Chardonnays are often potent, with lots of body and high alcohol, but equally can be more subtle and delicate in different hands, particularly from wineries towards the cooler southern end of the valley. Both are often matured in new oak barrels, to add complexity and toasty richness.

Sonoma Valley
ALSO TRY Syrah, Merlot, Cabernet Sauvignon

BEST FOR
Chardonnay, Pinot Noir, Zinfandel

Sonoma is not too far off Napa in terms of quality, but it is less well known. It's a little further west, so is closer to the sea, and, as such is more prone to the fogs and mists that help keep the wine-growing areas cool. This gives it more scope to play with a broad range of grape varieties. One particular area worth noting is the Russian River Valley, which is cool even for this region, and makes some elegant Chardonnays, chilled-out Zinfandels, sensuous Merlots and some of the best Pinot Noirs in the state.

SONOMA VALLEY
California

OTHER US STATES
worth exploring

Oregon

Relative to California, all other wine regions in the USA are pretty small. Yet Oregon is the state directly above California, and is one of the most exciting regions in the world producing Pinot Noir at the moment. It gives a unique and compelling expression of this most fascinating of red grapes. Oregon is a cool-climate region, so it's well-suited to Pinot Noir, which here can create wines of real interest and complexity, with herbal notes and hints of orange peel, cherries and many other intriguing flavours. The Willamette Valley to the north is currently the most promising of all Oregon's subregions – well worth hunting down a bottle. They also produce a fair bit of Pinot Gris, but to date, without such exciting results.

BEST FOR
Pinot Noir

Washington State

This state isn't the most obvious place to grow grapes; it gets virtually no rain at all in summer, and in winter the temperature can drop to -26˚C for days at a time. Although still hard to find in the UK, the wines of Washington State in the Pacific northwest, above Oregon, still deserve a mention: the state is the second most important US producer of wine, after California. In 1969, there were just two wineries in Washington; now there are over 600. The reds are particularly worth trying, and tend to be deeply coloured, with soft, rich fruit shot through with crisp acidity. This is a particularly successful spot for growing varietal Merlot, which is all too often a bit boring when unblended.

BEST FOR
Cabernet Sauvignon,
Syrah, Merlot,
Chardonnay,
Riesling

SOME GOOD WASHINGTON PRODUCERS
Château Ste Michelle, Col Solare, L'Ecole No 41, Snoqualmie Vineyards

SOME GOOD OREGON PRODUCERS
Firesteed, Beaux Frères, Domaine Drouhin Oregon, Sokol Blosser, Shea Wine Cellars, Rex Hill

New York State

New York State is a relative newcomer to winemaking. The majority of wineries here are less than 20 years old, and few make wines that are widely exported, but this situation is surely set to change as the quality increases. The two main areas are the Finger Lakes, near Lake Ontario to the north, and Long Island to the east. The former has a cool climate that favours German hybrid grape varieties above all, but there are also wineries producing some good-quality and good-value Rieslings. The Long Island region has a warmer, maritime climate where you can find subtle, elegant Chardonnays, Merlots, Cabernet Francs and Cabernet Sauvignons.

Virginia

The first vineyards of Virginia were planted in 1607, but despite President Thomas Jefferson's best efforts at his plantation, Monticello (where they now host a regional wine festival each year), quality winemaking has only really taken hold here in the last three decades. From only six wineries in 1979, Virginia now has dozens, and the state is producing some brilliant wines. Located halfway down the Atlantic coast, Virginia is a warm and relatively humid grape-growing area that has no trouble ripening varieties such as Merlot and Cabernet Franc; the wines made from them tend to be much fuller and richer in style compared to those made further north in New York State. These vibrant, fruity and often good-value wines aren't easy to find outside of the US, but they are being exported, and are worth a try if you can get your hands on them.

CANADA

The United States isn't the only country in North America to produce wine. Southern Canada is another cold but successful region for growing grapes on this continent, and its grapevines are always found next to large bodies of water – a fact that helps to regulate the vineyard microclimate . *Vinifera* vines are now being planted here, alongside the more usual hybrids, but Canadian producers are most famous for their Icewines (which use the same production method as German Eiswein – see page 133). Normally these cost a fortune, but in Canada Icewine is often relatively inexpensive to produce because the cold winter temperatures necessary to make it are so reliable.

Winemakers do produce some dry Riesling here, too, and even some good Pinot Noir. The extreme weather limits the number of styles of wine that can be made in this area, however, which means much of the wine drunk in the country is in fact imported. Canada is one of the few nations where domestically produced wines don't have a dominant share of the local market.

BEST FOR
Pinot Noir, Chardonnay, Riesling, Vidal (for icewine)

SOME GOOD CANADIAN PRODUCERS
Inniskillin Okanagan, Le Clos Jordanne

LATIN AMERICA

20

W inemaking in Latin America began in the sixteenth century, thanks to Spanish conquistadors taking vine cuttings to the Americas. It spread pretty quickly, and today the region makes a huge volume of wine – but it has only been of export quality since the late 1980s. The two main countries you need to know about are Argentina and Chile. If you're lucky, you might occasionally see the odd bottle from Brazil, Mexico and Uruguay, too.

ARGENTINA

Argentina is Latin America's biggest wine producer. A lot of excellent wine is made, but historically, the majority of grapes went into making weird sweet pink stuff for local consumption. After the dire internal political/economic situation of the 1950s-'80s, there was a pressing need to bring in foreign currency, so winemakers here started looking to export their wares. In order to create demand, these wines had to be good enough, so standards of production have shot up dramatically during the past 30 years. It's definitely a country to watch.

Today, the country creates great-value wines at the cheaper end of the scale, and world-class reds at the top.

Small wine-growing regions are dotted all over Argentina. It's frequently described as a vine-growing paradise: hot summer temperatures during the day, cool at night, but neither too extreme; rivers of pure meltwater running down from the Andes; well-drained, infertile soils. The most important area by far is Mendoza, to the west, which produces 70% of the country's wine. It's particularly good for reds: Argentina's strongest suit, especially its signature variety, Malbec.

Malbec is native to southwest France, where it's still found in red Bordeaux, and is also used to make the once-famous 'black wines' of Cahors, southeast of Bordeaux. It makes a full-bodied, concentrated, full-on red, and can be smooth, long and satisfying. In France, it creates good wines that tend to be serious; in Argentina they're fruitier and more vibrant. Particularly good from upper Mendoza and Salta.

Torrontés is the most famous white grape grown in Argentina. It makes delicious, medium- to full-bodied wines, highly aromatic and peachy, often with a touch of spice. It's similar to Viognier, but fresher and not so oily. Argentinean Torrontés can be really good value. Other whites are thinner on the ground, but they make a fair bit of decent Chardonnay in cooler, higher-altitude regions like La Rioja and Salta.

COMMON VARIETIES

RED
Cabernet Sauvignon, Malbec

WHITE
Chardonnay, Torrontés

SOME GOOD PRODUCERS
Bodega Catena Zapata, Trapiche, Masi (an Italian producer which has branched out here), Susana Balbo, Pascual Toso, Achaval Ferrer

CHILE

Like Argentina, Chile also had its viticulture imported by conquistadors, but, as a country, it has a lower output in terms of wine volume: around three-quarters that of Argentina. A very long, narrow country running north to south, Chile's extremities are either too hot or too cold for wine production, and only the middle part of the country has the right conditions for grape-growing. Within this band, however, are a number of different regions, all with their own specialities.

With the sea on one side and the Andes on the other, this is a particularly isolated part of the wine world – one reason why Chile was never affected by phylloxera (see page 12). As such, the majority of vines here grow on their original roots, not on the rootstocks of North American vines as in most of Europe. Whether this makes much difference to wine quality, though, is debatable.

Most Chilean wine exports are clean, fruity, lively varietals: the classic international Cabernet Sauvignon, Merlot, Syrah, Pinot Noir, as well as Chardonnay, Sauvignon Blanc and a little Riesling. But things aren't always quite as they seem...

After extensive scientific studies, it turns out that some of the 'Merlot' is, in fact, not Merlot at all, but a completely different red grape variety called Carmenère. Carmenère was widely grown in Bordeaux in the eighteenth century, but has now largely disappeared there. In Chile, however, it produces a full-bodied, gutsy red with notable blackcurrant and blackberry flavours and a particularly herbal, tomato-stalk or bell-pepper undertone. It can make good wines, and is a style unique to this country. Likewise, some Chilean 'Sauvignon Blanc' is one of a number of lesser-known varieties, including Sauvignonasse, Sauvignon Gris and Sauvignon Vert. The better vineyards are getting to the bottom of this conundrum now, and making sure what's planted in the ground equates to what's stated on the label.

There are a number of distinct wine regions in Chile, and each has its own special qualities:

SOME GOOD PRODUCERS
Concha y Toro, Errázuriz, Los Vascos, Casa Lapostolle, Coyam and Matetic

ACONCAGUA Produces good Sauvignon Blanc and Pinot Noir
CASABLANCA Produces impressive whites, particularly Sauvignon Blanc and Chardonnay
MAIPO Makes some of Chile's best Cabernet Sauvignon
RAPEL Produces great reds across the board: Merlot, Cab Sauv, Carmenère, Syrah
BÍO-BÍO AND MALLECO Make exciting Pinot Noir, Riesling and Chardonnay

CHILE

tin America

OTHER
latin american countries

Although Argentina and Chile are the biggest winemakers in Latin America, some wine is produced in numerous other countries produce. Mexico, Brazil and Uruguay all deserve a mention.

BRAZIL The third-largest wine producer in Latin America, Brazil makes mostly whites that are cultivated in the hilly areas in the south. It isn't the most obvious country to try to make good wine, as it's largely very wet; nonetheless, you see the occasional decent bottle – more and more so following investment from France and Italy. They even make decent sparklers.

MEXICO The fourth-largest country in terms of Latin American wine production. Most winemaking here is geared towards brandy, but some producers turn out good-quality table wines, particularly reds. In style, they're like a cross between Chile and California, made mostly from international varieties, especially Cabernet Sauvignon, Merlot, Cabernet Franc, Zinfandel and Malbec. Mexico also makes a fair bit of Petite Sirah: a dark, tannic, intense wine that has nothing to do with Syrah, but is known as Durif in Europe. Once a French grape variety, it's pretty much extinct there now, but it sometimes crops up in Australia.

URUGUAY OK, I'm not entirely sure it's worth including Uruguay, but just for interest, I'll tell you that they do make some decent Tannat here, which is a grape better known for producing Madiran, a wine made in a small French appellation southeast of Bordeaux. No prizes for guessing it's heavy on the tannin, but it does have the potential to make some good, plummy red wines (particularly in France). Not unlike Argentinean Malbec, though rarely as good. The usual gang of international varieties are also in attendance, some turning up in pretty good wines.

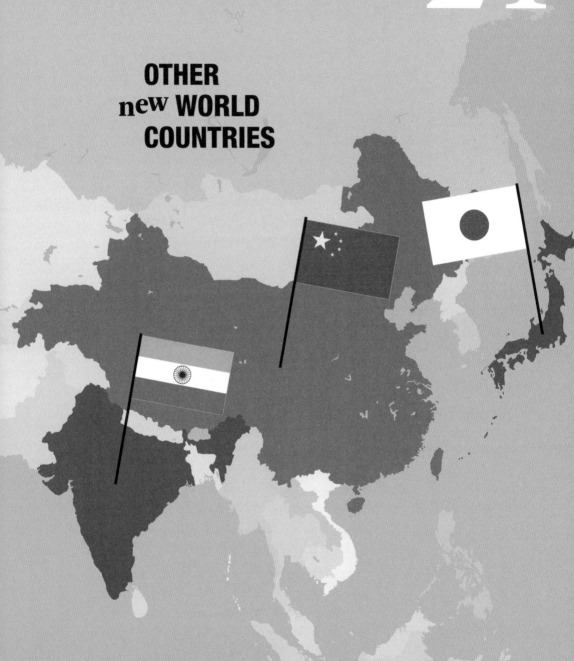

OTHER
new WORLD
COUNTRIES

21

Only a few other New World nations make wines you'll encounter outside their country of origin, but that is set to change as winemaking technology improves. For now, at least, the following constitute the 'Very New World' of wine.

INDIA, CHINA
and japan

India

India has been making wine for about 6,000 years, but only in the last 20 has it been any good. Most of the country is just too hot or too wet for grapes, so vineyards are planted mainly at high altitudes: up to 1,000m (3,280 feet) above sea level. Until the 1990s, you'd have had to settle for a bottle of Bangalore Blue rather than Cabernet Sauvignon. Historically, the country has been broadly anti-alcohol due to its Buddhist and Muslim heritage. Quality wines have only started to take off with the establishment of a more prosperous wine-drinking middle class.

SOME GOOD INDIAN PRODUCERS
Today, three main wineries create export-quality wines from international grapes: Sula Wines, Grover Vineyards and Château Indage (whose sparkling wine is actually pretty decent).

China

China produces bucketloads of wine, and most is drunk locally. Up-to-date wineries have existed only since the 1980s, so the modern industry is still in its infancy. A lot of investment has come from Western producers, and the standard is improving. Though the bulk is basic red table wine for local consumption, China is set to become a major new fine-wine producer. The most common grapes are Cabernet Sauvignon, Merlot, Cabernet Franc; Chardonnay and Riesling. A fair bit of land is still devoted to weird old Russian imports like Muscat Hamburg (better as a table grape) and Rkatsiteli (workhorse grape from Georgia).

Japan

Japan has been making wine since the Buddha Nyorai gave vines to a man in Honshu in AD 718. Either that, or they were imported by Portuguese missionaries – depends on who you ask. It's mostly too wet and humid for international varieties, so they grow unfamiliar ones like Koshu and Yamabudo, or American hybrids like Delaware and Concord. The Japanese drink more wine than any other Asian country. Only a third of wine drunk in Japan is locally made, so a lot is imported and often blended with local wines to make a kind of 'mixed-race wine'. The 100% Japanese stuff is more expensive.

22

OTHER wine STYLES

FORTIFIED
wines

F ortified wines are, not unlike Ebeneezer Goode in the eponymous song by The Shaman, very much maligned and misunderstood. Fashion is a fickle thing. Port, Sherry and Madeira have all been fashionable at some point, and rightly so. All have so many styles, grape varieties and extraordinary producers that each is a world of flavour waiting to be discovered. But because they're currently out of fashion, a good bottle is not so hard to reach. Some of the very best Sherries sell for around £70 a bottle compared to £2,000 for the best Bordeaux. Fortifieds are also the most varied of wines. They can be bone-dry or tooth-meltingly sweet, clear as water or deepest black, light and swift in the mouth or thick and gloopy, subtle and delicate or explosively flavoursome. They tend to be a touch higher in alcohol than typical dry table wines: Sherry is 15%–22% ABV; Madeira and Port around 20%. They repay exploring, so approach them with an open mind – you won't regret it.

Port

Port starts life like any other wine, but halfway through fermentation, brandy is added – about a fifth of the total volume. This spirit is 77% alcohol, and takes the overall ABV of the fermenting liquid up to around 20%. This level of alcohol stops the yeast from working, so not all the sugar turns to alcohol, which is why some natural sweetness remains.

The most common grapes used in red Ports are Touriga Nacional, Touriga Francesa, Tinta Cão, Tinta Roriz and Tinta Barroca, grown along the Douro Valley in Portugal, on terraces that snake horizontally along steep hillsides overlooking the river Douro. It's bloody hot, bloody beautiful – and bloody hard to work; the soil is basically granite. Port comes in many different guises, but there are three main styles: white, tawny, and red.

White Port
White Port can be dry or sweet, and is made mostly from Rabigato, Malvasia Fina and Malvasia Rei grapes. It's typically fairly sweet, golden and viscous with around 20% ABV. Nice chilled, with a grapey, peachy flavour, but it's particularly refreshing with tonic water (three parts tonic to one part Port), ice and a sprig of mint.

Tawny Port

There are three types of tawny Ports.

1 **FINE TAWNY** isn't fine. It's made by blending ruby Port with white Port, and is sold mainly to French truckers. Better avoided.

2 **AGED TAWNY** has been aged a stated number of years (ten, 20, 30 or 40) and is one of the finest drinks known to man. Matured in small oak barrels, it develops fairly quickly due to gentle oxidation through the wood. A clear, brown-red colour, it takes on more nutty, woody, dried-fruit character the older it gets. It can be hugely complex, with dozens of flavours, and goes well with desserts, including dark chocolate. Drink it chilled or at room temperature. Once opened, it lasts for a good month in the fridge with a cork in.

3 **COLHEITA** essentially translates as 'harvest', and means a tawny Port from a single vintage. *Colheitas* are very similar to aged tawnies, but bear the character of the year in which they were made. They have to be aged for at least seven years before release, and can last for 60 years or longer in good vintages.

Red Port

There are six types here: ruby, special reserve, late-bottled vintage (LBV), crusted, single-quinta and vintage.

1 **RUBY PORT** is aged in large vats, then bottled fairly young. It makes a powerfully flavoured, deep purple-ruby drink with lots of primary fruit flavour and spirity alcohol. Some can be decent, if rarely that complex.

2 **SPECIAL RESERVE** is made with more care from better fruit and aged longer. It should be more refined and complex, although it's still a fairly simple drink.

3 **LATE-BOTTLED VINTAGE** is made from the fruit of one harvest, aged in large wooden vats for five or six years, then bottled, ready to drink. This and all other Ports mentioned so far don't require decanting. LBVs can be good-quality, good-value drinks, typically around £9–£20. Not bad for what is a complex, long, balanced, sumptuous wine. The best are 'traditional' or 'unfiltered' and will state this on the label. If old, these unfiltered versions can create some sediment in the bottom of the bottle.

4 **CRUSTED PORT** spends more time in bottle and less in vat than LBV, and throws a bigger deposit, so needs decanting.

5 **SINGLE-QUINTA** This is is when the wines really start to shine. *Quinta* means estate, so essentially it's a single-estate Port, made from the grapes of a single harvest. Each estate has its own character and style. Basically a vintage Port, but in a year that isn't 'declared', and from a single estate rather than a blend.

6 **VINTAGE** Ports are made only in the best years: only three each decade on average will be 'declared' as a vintage. Traditionally, Port houses declare a vintage on St George's Day (April 23). Vintage Ports can be things of awesome power, beauty and longevity. Taylor's Vintage 1934, for instance, isn't over the hill yet. Don't even think about touching a vintage Port until 15–20 years after the vintage; much before this and they're just too intense and tannic – they need time to mellow and balance out before showing their best.

One last thing about Port: if you're looking for a good drink with subtle but robust flavours that go perfectly with a cigar, this is it.

Sherry

'Sherry' is a bastardization of 'Jerez', the region in southern Spain where it's made. All but some sweet styles come from one grape variety: Palomino. The best grow on brilliant white *albariza* soil. Styles range from pale and fresh to dark and luxurious. It's not the most straightforward wine, so let's get the main styles mapped out.

Sherry types

FINO & MANZANILLA

• Always dry, pale white wines of around 15% ABV, low acidity, little fruit (a hint of apple or lemon) and a yeasty aroma and flavour. Both are bone-dry and matured in barrels under a layer of yeast called *flor*, which prevents oxidation.
• Manzanilla must be made in the town of Sanlúcar de Barrameda. It often has camomile hints and a slightly salty tang. Finos are a touch more neutral.

TRY THEM WITH
Salads, seafood and salami. Good on their own or before a meal, too.

AMONTILLADO

• True amontillados are beautiful; 'amontillado medium' denotes an inferior sweetened blend. The real thing is made by aging fino or manzanilla until it tastes nuttier and more complex. Always dry.
• Deeper in colour, often with hazelnut and woody flavours.
• Starts the same way as a fino or manzanilla, but the flor dies and the wine ages in the presence of oxygen to get that distinctive Sherry flavour.

TRY IT WITH
Pâtés, cold meats, cheese; also game birds

OLOROSO

• Richer still; deeper colour than an amontillado; smooth with a walnut flavour.
• Aged in the presence of oxygen, with strong flavours.
• Around 18%–20% ABV, more as they age. Most olorosos are dry, but some sweet ones, called sweet or rich oloroso or *oloroso abocado*, can be wonderful.

TRY IT WITH
Sweet ones: treacle tart, pecan pie, or any dessert with dried fruit. Dry ones: hot or cold savoury dishes.

PALO CORTADO

• Always dry. Like a cross between an amontillado and an oloroso. The most complex, interesting dry Sherry of all. Can be pricy, but it will really reveal some fascinating flavours.

TRY IT WITH
Similar foods to an amontillado, but is often best on its own.

PEDRO XIMÉNEZ (PX)

• Nothing like the other styles. Intensely sweet, black, gloopy wine made from shrivelled Pedro Ximénez (*PEHdro heMEHneth*) grapes. It tastes like liquidized Christmas pudding: dried fruit and a touch of toffee or molasses.

TRY IT
Poured over vanilla ice cream. Easiest dessert in the world and you'll look dead fancy.

CREAM & PALE CREAM

• Sweet. This is the stuff your granny drinks. Just don't bother.

Madeira

Madeira's kind of like Sherry but with higher acidity and often a hint of smokiness. It isn't quite as varied in style, and yes, it's made in Madeira, the little rocky island off the coast of Portugal. It usually has flavours of dried fruit (raisins, prunes and figs), orange peel, and hazelnuts or walnuts. The easiest way to approach it is in three categories: three-year-old 'finest' and five-year-old 'reserve'; ten-year-old 'special reserve' and 15-year-old 'extra reserve'; and vintage.

Once Madeira is opened, stick the cork back and it will last almost indefinitely.

1 THREE-YEAR-OLD 'FINEST', FIVE-YEAR-OLD 'RESERVE'

Madeiras range from basic to ultra-high quality. This is the basic stuff. It's not that interesting as a drink but is a useful cooking ingredient (add a glass when roasting a bird or making gravy). Made from the widely planted Tinta Negra Mole grape (versatile but rarely exciting), it comes in four styles: dry, medium-dry, medium-sweet (or medium-rich), and sweet (or rich). These should be on the label.

2 TEN-YEAR-OLD 'SPECIAL RESERVE', 15-YEAR-OLD 'EXTRA RESERVE'

These come in the same four sweetness styles listed above, but production methods are more stringent and one of the four 'noble' grape varieties is used for each style. Dry is made of Sercial; medium-dry of Verdelho; medium-sweet of Bual; and sweet, of Malvasia (aka Malmsey). Quality at this level can be very good.

3 VINTAGE

Made from the fruit of a single harvest. Prices don't get as high as they should, considering the quality of this wine. It's made from the same 'noble' varieties, and sometimes from funny old grapes you don't see anymore, like Terrantez or Bastardo. These can be powerful wines with fascinating flavours and extraordinary length. Vintage Madeiras are the longest-lived wines in the world; it's not unusual to see wines for sale from the late 1700s, often for only a few hundred pounds per bottle – not cheap, but, when you consider that the peasant who crushed the grapes probably lived at a time when everyone wore white curly wigs, it takes on an almost transcendental quality.

SOME GOOD MADEIRA PRODUCERS
D'Olivera, Barbeito, Henriques & Henriques, Blandy

MAKING MADEIRA
Madeira lasts so long due to the *estufa* process: the wine is heated to age it and add flavour. In cheap versions, hot (40–50 ˚C) water runs in pipes through wine-filled concrete tanks for around three months. In the ten- and 15-year-old versions, the wine is put in wooden casks, and heated by boilers (30–40 ˚C) for six to 12 months. Vintage wines are stored in small wooden casks under the roofs of lodges heated by the sun – sometimes for up to 20 years. Before they're heated, the wines are fortified with 95% grape spirit.

OTHER WINE STYLES:
dessert wines

Sweet or dessert wines are some of the most varied, interesting and best-value wines on the planet. Next time you see a half-bottle in the shop, give it a try.

Muscats

Many sweet wines are made from the Muscat grape, especially in France (Muscat de Beaumes-de-Venise) but also Spain (Moscatel de Valencia) and Portugal (Moscatel de Setúbal). These range from the average to delicious gems. They tend to be white, sweet and grapey, sometimes with a hint of tangerine. As a group, these *vins doux naturels* (natural sweet wines) are made in a similar way to Port. Often fairly cheap.

Sweet reds

Sweet red wines, often made in the south of France, are made in the same way as white *vins doux naturels*. The most common appellations are Banyuls, Maury and Rivesaltes, made mainly from Grenache. Not unlike slightly fruitier versions of Port, with powerful fresh and dried black and red fruits at the fore.

New World

Most New World sweet wines are *vins doux naturels*, though many are also made in the Port and Sherry method. Impossible to generalize, here, so it's best to ask the guy or girl in the wine shop what they're like.

Sauternes

SOME GOOD SAUTERNES PRODUCERS
Sensibly priced examples come from Château Bastor-Lamontange, Château d'Arche, Château Haut-Bergeron and Château Monteils.

The most famous sweet wine of Bordeaux, probably of all dessert wines, is made from two varieties: Sémillon and Sauvignon Blanc, affected by noble rot (see page 133). Sauternes has intense apricot and peach/pineapple fruit coupled with a hint of marmalade or mushroom. It can last for decades in bottle, and some of these wines are highly sought-after and eye-wateringly expensive. One of the most famous wines in the world, Château d'Yquem, is a Sauternes, and typically sells for around £300 a bottle. Rarely the best value at the cheaper end, Sauternes's still worth exploring; it can be incredibly long, complex and delicious.

Alsace

Alsace's sweet wines aren't commonly seen outside France – a shame because they can be a real treat. They should say *vendage tardive* on the label ('late harvest': i.e. the grapes were very overripe and sweet) or *sélection des grains nobles* (made from picking berries affected by noble rot). They can be made from Riesling, Pinot Gris, Pinot Blanc, Gewurztraminer or Muscat.

Vin santo

Silky-sweet wine from Italy with high acidity and dried-fruit flavours such as raisins and figs. Made from semi-dried grapes, then aged in tiny barrels which mature the wine quickly and add to the slightly oxidative aromas.

GERMANY
Most of the best German wines have some degree of sweetness. They're usually made from Riesling, and benefit from its pure, clean fruit flavours. Made with a different ethos to most other sweet wines, they're covered in the Germany chapter (see page 133). Dessert wines have *Beerenauslese* or *Trockenbeerenauslese* on the label.

Tokáji

The most famous wine from Hungary is made largely from two indigenous varieties: Furmint and Hárslevelu, which will have seen some noble rot (see page 133). These fascinating wines are golden, with a good level of sweetness, but also a marked acidity that keeps them interesting. Flavours of apricots, marmalade, mushrooms and dried fruits are what to expect.

Málaga

Fortified wine from southern Spain that is increasingly rare. Málaga ranges from dry to sweet, and 15%–23% ABV. They are made mostly from Pedro Ximénez.

Marsala

A fortified wine from Sicily, once common, now rarely seen. It comes in a vast array of sweetness, colours, flavours, etc., and is often made from dodgy grape varieties. Most (but not all) Marsala these days is really only worth cooking with.

Liqueur muscat

One of the best sweet wines of Australia. It tastes like thick, liquid toffee, with grapes and raisins on the nose, and can be a glorious. Deserves to be better known.

APPENDIX 1:
visiting english wineries

'English Wine' used to conjure up images of a bearded, sandal-wearing retired hobbyist making something out of nettles. Today, a lot of good English (and Welsh) wine is being produced, in red, white, rosé and sparkling versions. What the UK climate's best for, though, is sparkling wine, because grapes don't have to be perfectly ripe to create a good result. UK sparklers are usually lean, fresh, dry and crisp. They're rarely as rich as the toastiest French styles, but that isn't always what you want. Still reds tend to be light and subtle, and still whites vary from crisp and aromatic to medium-sweet and floral. Many larger UK wineries are open to visitors, and many have visitor centres offering tours and tastings, and even restaurants and bed and breakfast cottages. Here are some of the best.

Bolney Vineyards, West Sussex

Bolney grows 11 different types of grapes, but unusually, specializes in red wines. These are some of my favourite English reds. The Pinot Noir in particular is very good: light and delicate in style but well made and worth sniffing out.
TRY THE Foxhole Vineyards Pinot Noir
VISITS? Yes, book online
WEBSITE www.bolneywineestate.co.uk

Gusbourne, Kent

You'll find only the three Champagne grapes on this estate in Kent. Their sparkling wines are a little richer than some of the intensely mineral styles from producers such as Nyetimber.
TRY THE Brut Reserve NV
VISITS? Email visit@gusbourne.com
WEBSITE www.gusbourne.com

Camel Valley, Cornwall

Established in 1989 by ex-RAF pilot Bob Lindo, Camel Valley's wines are now made by his son Sam. They've won many awards – and not just when pitted against other English wines, but when competing against other countries, too. Eleven different still and sparkling wines are made here.
TRY THE 'Cornwall' Brut 2009
VISITS? Yes, but you have to book online
WEBSITE www.camelvalley.com

Ridgeview, East Sussex

Ridgeview's sparkling wines are brilliant. Not only do they look good (a rare thing among English wines), the wine quality is fantastic – which is why it is often served by the Queen at Buckingham Palace to visiting dignitaries.
TRY THE Bloomsbury Cuvée Merret 2009
VISITS? Drop in to taste and buy a few bottles any day but Sunday or Bank Holidays. You can arrange tours by appointment.
WEBSITE www.ridgeview.co.uk

Nyetimber, West Sussex

The largest vineyard in the UK (438 acres), and probably the most famous of all the UK's sparkling wines. Nyetimber makes very elegant sparklers that are lean, minerally and very dry.
TRY THE Blanc de Blancs 2001
VISITS? No
WEBSITE www.nyetimber.com

Three Choirs, Gloucestershire

A large, well-established winery on the Gloucestershire/Herefordshire border. Three Choirs mainly makes still whites, with a bit of red and rosé, chiefly from German varieties and unusual hybrids.

TRY THE Bacchus 2009
VISITS? Yes, just turn up. Tours 11am or 3pm, Monday to Saturday
WEBSITE www.three-choirs-vineyards.co.uk

Hush Heath, Kent

This winery only makes rosé, a sparkling and a still one, both from a blend of the three main Champagne grapes. Although it has only been produced for a few years, the sparkling Balfour Brut is making waves and winning big awards.

TRY THE Balfour Brut Rosé 2005
VISITS? Yes, from April to September, one Thursday per month, by appointment
WEBSITE www.hushheath.com

Breaky Bottom, East Sussex

Going since 1974, Breaky grows mostly Seyval Blanc. The variety is common in England and used to make still wine, but here it goes into one of the best sparklers in the UK.

TRY THE Sparkling Brut 2006
VISITS? Yes, by appointment
WEBSITE www.breakybottom.co.uk

Chapel Down, Kent

Chapel Down makes a wide range of wines, but specializes in sparkling and still whites. Though there are a lot of English sparkling wines I love to drink, finding still wines is more difficult; Chapel Down tends to be a good bet.

TRY THE Sparkling Pinot Chardonnay 2006
VISITS? Yes, open seven days a week
WEBSITE www.chapeldown.com

Astley, Worcestershire

Once the world's most northern vineyard, Astley makes some very good whites. This is a small operation and not terribly well known, but it has been running for over 30 years.

TRY THE Kerner 'Veritas' 2009
VISITS? Yes, tours by appointment
WEBSITE www.astley-vineyards.co.uk

INSIDER TIP

Wiston Estate Winery, West Sussex

One of the most exciting new wine ventures in the UK. Wiston Estate is a state-of-the-art winery set up in 2008 by one of the UK's most promising winemakers. Using Champagne grape varieties on chalky soil similar to that in the Champagne region itself, this is one to keep a close eye on.

TRY THE Wiston Estate Sparkling 2009
VISITS? Not yet
WEBSITE www.wistonestate.com

DON'T BE FOOLED! They sound similar, but English Wine and British Wine are very different animals. English Wines are wines made in England, like the ones above. 'British Wine' is the official term for an alcoholic drink made from imported grape juice or concentrate from anywhere in the world and fermented in the UK, often to a pretty nasty effect. The end result tends to be similar in strength to sherry and medium sweet. Avoid.

APPENDIX 2:
buying tips for readers in the uk

There have been a lot of changes to the high street over the past five years or so, not least when it comes to buying wine. Popping out to the off-licence was once the standard way of getting your hands on a bottle of wine in the UK. Off-licences used to be a common feature of every town and city centre, but they're now a dying breed. First Unwins closed its shops in 2005. Then First Drinks, with Threshers, Wine Rack, The Local and Haddows, bit the dust in 2009. And most recently, Oddbins closed its doors in 2011, though has since reopened a handful of shops.

Majestic Wine Warehouse is still going strong with its successful model of out-of-town shops, easy parking and low prices. It has a decent range, considering its size, and there are often some good-value wines to be found. Sadly, though, you have to buy a minimum of six or even 12 bottles, so it's not a viable option if you're on foot or en route to a party.

UK supermarkets are a mixed bag. Some have very good ranges, but others are very bad. At the moment, E H Booth in particular is brilliant; Waitrose is very good; Marks & Spencer is good but sometimes it stocks wine with different labels that are exclusive to it, so it's not always easy to make a selection. Tesco and Sainsbury's are both OK.

The best way to get hold of really interesting wines is at independent merchants, and with the demise of the big chains, there have been more and more popping up of late. You don't necessarily have to visit in person if you don't have one nearby; most can arrange local or national delivery. This means there's no need to put up with average wines when you can get a mixed case delivered to your door.

Here is a brief, but by no means exhaustive, list of independent wine merchants worth looking up. Most cities will only have one or two, but, because of its size, London has a number of good ones.

London
- Armit, W11
- Bibendum, NW1
- Clarion Wines, W4
- Green & Blue, SE22
- Harvey Nicholls, SW1
- Highbury Vintners, N5
- Howard Ripley, SW13
- Jeroboams (eight locations)
- Justerini & Brooks, SW1
- Last Drop Wines, SW10
- Lea & Sandeman (four locations)
- Moreno Wines, W9
- O W Loeb, SE1
- Philglas & Swiggot (three locations)
- Roberson Wine, W14
- The Sampler, SW7 & N1
- Swig, NW3
- Uncorked, EC2
- Vagabond, SW6
- Wilkinson Vintners, NW1
- The Winery, W9
- Wimbledon Wine Cellars (three locations)

Bristol & Somerset
- Great Western Wines, Bath
- Reid Wines, Bristol

Cambridgeshire
- Cambridge Wine Merchants, Cambridge
- Noel Young, Cambridge

Cheshire
- DeFine Food and Wine, Sandiway, Cheshire

East & West Midlands
- Connolly's, Birmingham, West Midlands
- Gauntley's, Nottingham, East Midlands
- Nickolls & Perks, Stourbridge,
  West Midlands

East & West Sussex
- The Butler's Wine Cellar, Brighton,
  East Sussex
- David Kibble Wines, Arundel, West Sussex
- Four Walls, Chichester, West Sussex

Greater Manchester & Lancashire
- D. Byrne, Clitheroe, Lancashire
- Hanging Ditch, Manchester

Hampshire & Surrey
- Caviste, Overton, Hampshire
- Les Caves de Pyrène, Guildford
- Imbibros, Godalming, Surrey

Kent
- The Secret Cellar, Tunbridge Wells

Oxfordshire & Wiltshire
- The Oxford Wine Company, Oxford
- Stevens Garnier, Oxford
- Yapp Brothers, Mere, Wiltshire

Norfolk
- Harper Wells, Norwich

Northern Ireland
- James Nicholson, Crossgar, County Down

Scotland
- Invararity, Glasgow
- Raeburn Fine Wines, Edinburgh
- Villeneuve Wines, Edinburgh
- WoodWinters, Edinburgh

Shropshire
- Bentley's, Ludlow

Suffolk
- Adnams, Southwold

Yorkshire
- House of Townend, Hull
- Wrightson and Company, Richmond,
  North Yorkshire

Wales
- Vinomondo, Conwy

Other
- Tanners also has several branches
  around the Midlands and Wales

MAIL-ORDER COMPANIES

There's one other way to get hold of your vino, and that's through mail-order companies. The biggest in the UK at the moment is Direct Wines, which owns Laithwaites and several newspaper wine clubs. I have heard good reports about Naked Wines, and The Wine Society is excellent.

INDEX

FINAL WORD

Exploring all the weird and wonderful corners of the world of wine is one of the most amazing things your tongue will ever do. So many people go to galleries and music venues to feast their eyes and ears on incredible sights and sounds, but smells and tastes can be just as extraordinary, thought-provoking, inspiring and beautiful, and nowhere will you find this more than in a good bottle of wine. There are an endless number of different ones to try, all renewed afresh each year with a new vintage – and they get you amusingly wasted. And all you need to do is pull the cork out and pour. What am I waiting for? I'm off down the wine shop... See you there!

ACKNOWLEDGEMENTS

In many ways, this has been a collaborative project, and I owe a huge debt of gratitude to the following people, many of whom offered their expertise for little more than a few beers. Good friends indeed.

To my dad, for his boundless encouragement and Franglais lessons. To my mum, the secret hedonist, for teaching me all about food and wine. To my sister Julie for all the good advice. To Nikki Engelbach, Dr. Nicky Headlam and Dr. Tom Wormald, for their help with the structure. To Patricia Stefanowicz MW and Anne Krebiehl (nearly MW!), for helping to verify the factual information. To Tony Hay, for help with photography, and to Sam Hails, for design and typesetting the original version. To Stephen Skelton MW, Mark Hanks and Liz & Iain Chapple, for information on publishing. To Anna Kerrane and Ben Pile, for help with graphics and web. To Anne Furniss, for giving the book a chance; to Jamie Ambrose, Mark McGinlay, Simon Davis and Katherine Case at Quadrille, for helping to create the finished article. And last but not least, to Louisa Bassant, for her endless support, advice and patience, and being the perfect partner in crime! A massive thank you to you all.